PRAISE FOR

SERVING GOD ~~AND~~ WITH MONEY

In a world shaped by financial stress and material ambition, *Serving God with Money* offers a refreshing, faith-based approach to personal finance. Through the relatable journey of Geoff and Janice Wilson, Frank J. Aloi shows how biblical principles can transform everyday financial struggles into meaningful opportunities for growth and service.

Blending storytelling with practical wisdom, this inspiring guide challenges readers to honor God not just with their treasure, but with their time and talent as well. It's a call to live generously, steward faithfully, and discover purpose in every financial decision.
—C Elliott Haverlack, author of *"Unbundling It", "Firestarter" and "From Fear to Fulfillment"*

***

Whether you are new to the concepts of Biblical Finance, if you have been practicing this approach to your stewardship for a long time, or even if you simply can use some encouragement in your financial journey, Mr. Aloi has delivered a thoughtful resource and a very accessible platform for study, planning, and conversation.

Mr. Aloi's clarity in discussing key ideas in *Serving God with Money* helps to give focus to the practical matters and challenges of personal finance in our world today. Through supporting Biblical financial concepts with scripture passages and meaningful interpretation, Mr. Aloi provides faithful motivation and dispels common misunderstandings, while relating these truths to likeable characters in whom we can see ourselves.

Serving God with Money is an effective approach for couples and families to enter into, or continue to grow in, stewardship, and its accessibility, accompanied by clear and easy-to-use tools, is a firm foundation for small group study or seminars in churches and other faith-based organizations.
—David M. Hollenbaugh, Executive Director,
Slippery Rock University Foundation

***

Frank Aloi offers a wonderful new resource in *Serving God with Money.* He has created an amazingly accessible presentation of financial principles and sound interpretation of biblical texts that support these principles.

Unlike other books presenting an alternative approach towards managing money, *Serving God with Money* draws the reader in through a simple story with relatable characters. The book invites the reader to follow the experience of three couples who attend a financial seminar led by the pastor of their church. Through these couples, Aloi presents a spectrum of financial challenges, and examples of how following biblical principles for handling money can improve people's lives and increase their capacity to add value to their community through generosity and service.

This book will provide hope for those seeking guidance and realistic expectations for those who have limited resources. The material is clearly organized and easy to understand. Through the character of Pastor Pete Aloi provides and explains how to use helpful practical resources which are available to readers through links to online materials.

Serving God with Money is a unique and valuable addition to the available resources on biblical financial principles. The simple narrative presentation and thoughtful organization makes it an excellent choice for personal reading, small groups, or congregational stewardship campaigns.
—Rev. John Porter, Transitional Ministry Specialist and ordained minister of *Word and Sacrament in the Presbyterian Church (PCUSA)*

***

Serving God with Money by Frank J. Aloi is an accessible and timely resource that speaks to the real struggles many believers face today. With the warmth and insight of a Christian heart, Aloi meets readers where they are, acknowledging the very real tension between faith and finances that can quietly take hold of our lives. Through a relatable story and clear, scripture-rooted teaching, he reminds us how even sincere desires can drift into stress, debt, and uncertainty. Rather than stoking a sense of guilt or quick answers, this book invites readers into a prayerful and honest examination of stewardship, life priorities, and faithful trust, all grounded in God's Word and reflected through everyday family life.

What sets this book apart is its balance of conviction and grace. Aloi not only explains what the Bible says about money; he also shows how to faithfully live into practical ways of budgeting, saving, giving, and spending—with clarity and hope. *Serving God with Money* is not a call to pursue wealth, but to follow God with our finances in the faithful hope of deepening discipleship. Whether read on your own, with your spouse, or within a small group, this book brings clarity, strengthens faith, and guides the reader toward peace in one of the most sensitive and challenging areas of Christian life.

—Rev. Dr. Tom Harmon, Executive Presbyter,
Beaver-Butler Presbytery (PCUSA)

***

I SO appreciate *Serving God with Money*! Frank Aloi has written an important book for anyone wanting to take a next step in bringing their whole life in harmony with God's call. He helps us understand that money and finances aren't separate from our faith and spirituality, but an intimate part of how we live with and serve God. It's written so simply, accessibly, yet profoundly. Frank isn't just writing for others. He writes out of his own striving to balance his faith, is finances, and his vocation in financial guidance. You will find this book immensely helpful.

—The Rev. Dr. Graham Standish—pastor, spiritual director, therapist, teacher, writer, speaker (www.ngrahamstandish.org)

SERVING GOD ~~AND~~ WITH MONEY

A Journey Towards Faith, Finance, and Fulfillment

FRANK J. ALOI

Published by KHARIS PUBLISHING, an imprint of KHARIS MEDIA LLC.

ISBN-13: 978-1-63746-687-2

ISBN-10: 1-63746-687-0

Library of Congress Control Number: 2026935203

All KHARIS PUBLISHING products are available at special quantity discounts for bulk purchases for sales promotions, premiums, fund-raising, and educational needs. For details, contact:

Kharis Media LLC
Tel: +1 (331) 312-2376
support@kharispublishing.com
www.kharispublishing.com

TABLE OF CONTENTS

CHAPTER

1

HOW DID WE GET HERE?

"This bill is higher than last month!" Geoff Wilson exclaimed as he slumped in the chair of his home office. The winter in Pittsburgh had been unusually cold, and heating costs were biting into everyone's pockets. The Wilsons, as Geoff had just discovered, were no exception.

Geoff's wife Janice entered the room, having overheard her husband's exasperated statement. "Is everything alright?" she asked, her tone gentle but curious.

"No, Janice. It doesn't seem like we're getting ahead at all. I don't understand it. I think we should be doing better with our money."

"Well, I know that we're really good at spending it, honey", Janice responded.

These moments had become a common occurrence in the Wilson family household. Although Geoff and Janice appeared to have it all together. Both were working full-time now; Janice had returned to her position at the local bank a few years earlier and their children, now teenagers, were old enough to take care of themselves. Geoff and Janice no longer worried about leaving them alone at home for a few hours without parental supervision.

The couple's expectation was that Janice's salary would set them on a steady path toward retirement. At least, that was the plan. But somehow, even with her salary coming in, the Wilsons were still struggling financially.

In addition to regular monthly bills, Geoff had planned to save for their upcoming vacation in Florida. He was determined not to repeat the old cycle of embarking on a vacation and then spending several months afterward paying off the credit card bill. In fact, they had just finished paying off last year's vacation the prior month.

The couple had also wanted to start saving for college as their children were reaching their teenage years. But month after month, the plan slipped further away because there was never enough money left by the time all the bills were paid.

Janice sat in the chair across from Geoff's office desk, recognizing that he was frustrated at the apparent lack of a solution to their financial problems.

"Something has to change," Geoff muttered, pressing his forehead into his palms. He looked up and stared into his wife's eyes. Then he lowered his head, shaking it slowly back and forth. When he finally looked up, he asked wearily, "Honey, how did we get here?"

***

The following Sunday, Janice announced "Everyone, it's time to leave!" Her voice reverberated through the house, prompting Geoff to glance at the clock on the wall. "Why does every Sunday morning go by so fast?" he thought to himself. Church had been part of the family's Sunday routine for years, but between Kayla's soccer games and Steven's touring baseball team tournaments, his attendance was less than stellar. This caused Janice to attend many Sunday services without her husband.

"I would like to be there before the prelude ends!" she added, hoping that a stern second order might finally rally the troops.

Slowly, Kayla and Steven stomped down the stairs, reaching the bottom just as their father appeared. Geoff stood at the top of the staircase, furiously trying to put on his tie.

"Maybe I should just go without one," he muttered. "I like that tie," Janice responded, hoping that a few positive words might change his mind.

The family soon piled into their new Porsche SUV, the latest addition to the Wilson clan. The plush leather seats were heated, which offered some comfort against the bitter chill of another frigid morning.

The drive to Living Water Church took only 10 minutes, and Geoff noticed the filled parking lot in the distance as he turned onto the road leading to the church. After dropping off Janice and the kids near the entrance, he circled around to the far side of the church building and pulled into one of the few empty slots.

Geoff chuckled to himself. "I guess Pastor Pete is packing the pews."

Pastor Pete Martin had arrived at the church the previous spring, right around the time the kids' schedule began filling up with Sunday morning sporting events. Although Geoff had spoken with him a few times, Janice was much more familiar with their new minister.

As Geoff walked into the Church atrium, he couldn't help but notice the energy in the room. The place felt alive. He also noticed that many of the faces were unfamiliar, people who had not been around back when he attended regularly.

While Kayla and Steven headed off to their youth group gathering, Geoff and Janice joined the adult fellowship, each grabbing a cup of coffee and a scone.

"Hey, Geoff!" was the remark behind him. As he turned around, Geoff realized that it was Mike Bennett. "How are you, man? I haven't seen you here in a couple of months!"

Geoff didn't quite know how to respond to that statement. Indeed, it was true that he had missed several Sunday services, but the verbal expression of this reminder made him a bit uncomfortable.

"Yeah, Mike. We've been busy, but things are quieting down now. We hope to be here more often."

"Well, it's good to see you, my friend! He extended his hand and Geoff returned the handshake. I'm sure we will be bumping into each other again!"

The family regrouped just as the worship service was about to begin. Geoff looked around and realized that seating was already at a premium, but he managed to find a few available seats together near the back of the bustling congregation.

As worship time approached, the announcements for "What's happening at Living Water Church" scrolled across the large projection screens on either side of the altar. Between them hung the cross of

Christ. Once the announcements ended, Pastor Pete strolled up to the pulpit.

"Before we begin worship, I have one additional announcement, he said. I want to remind you that our small group seminar, "Serving God with Money", begins next Sunday after the worship service. If you are interested, there is still time to sign up in the church atrium at the central information area."

Geoff leaned over to Janice and whispered, "Great, now God wants more money from us." His comment drew a smirk and a chuckle from him, but Janice quietly scolded him "Geoff, please!"

Despite scoffing at the seminar's title, Geoff found the worship service uplifting. The message centered on Jesus' model of evangelism in John Chapter 4. For a moment, it almost made him want to come back the following Sunday. But then his thoughts drifted to the endless list of unfinished tasks, and he quickly refocused on the week ahead.

CHAPTER

2

THE INVITATION

A few days later, Janice entered her craft room only to find that the ceiling light was acting up again. Frustrated, she called out to her husband, "The light keeps shutting off by itself, and then it starts blinking!"

Geoff responded, "Maybe it's time to buy a new one", not realizing that this suggestion would be added to his to-do list.

"You're going to the grocery store anyway today, Janice reminded him. "Just stop by the hardware store on your way there."

Rather than argue that his itinerary for the day was filling up quickly, Geoff decided to climb into the Porsche and drive to the local hardware store.

As he entered the massive complex, Geoff spotted the "Lighting" sign and followed it down to the correct aisle. There were many ceiling lights to choose from and the selection quickly became overwhelming, but he eventually found a fixture similar to the one in Janice's room. "It's the safe bet," he muttered to himself, grabbing one off the shelf before heading toward the checkout area at the front of the store.

As he turned, however, a familiar face was staring at him from a few feet away – it was Pastor Pete, smiling and nodding in his direction.

"Your wife send you here too?" the pastor asked with a grin.

Geoff admitted that he was there at Janice's request to fix her ceiling light. As he described the situation, Pastor Pete held up his hand and offered a few suggestions.

"Maybe a wire came loose? Did you recently replace the bulb in that light?"

"I don't know. I usually don't try to fix things," Geoff replied. I find it easier just to buy a new one and throw the old one out. Then I hire someone to come by and install it.

There was a brief pause before Pastor Pete nodded toward the box in Geoff's hands and asked "Is that the style you're looking for?"

"Janice likes this type of light; it's what she has now," Geoff said, looking down at the box in his hands. The price tag, a bold $149, caught his eyes, and he gave Pastor Pete a sheepish grin.

"Well Geoff, if I were you, I would consider checking the wires or trying a different bulb first."

Geoff stared down for a moment, then lifted his eyes to meet the Pastor's. "Maybe you're right. I can always come back if that doesn't work."

"Yes, you can. And if you need any help, just give me a call. I do several of these 'fix it' jobs around the house myself."

Geoff left the store without the light, jumped back into the Porsche and drove home. He was never one for DIY home repairs when he could easily hire someone to do it. However, emboldened by Pastor Pete's encouragement, he decided he would give it a try himself.

When Geoff arrived home, he explained his plan to Janice, which caught her by surprise. "Wait, you're going to fix the light yourself? That doesn't sound like something you would do. She couldn't hold back a smirk, though offered a bit of encouragement. "But go right ahead and give it a try!"

Geoff grabbed one of his iPads and opened the YouTube app. Searching for "fixing a ceiling light," he found several videos that walked him through the process.

"First, turn off the circuit breaker for the room in your breaker panel," instructed the DIY guide in the video. "Then, unscrew the light fixture and check that the wires are still connected." Following the steps carefully, he discovered that the two black wires were a bit loose, and so he twisted them together so that they were tighter. A few minutes later, with the wires tightened, Geoff reassembled the light fixture.

It was now the moment of truth. He turned the breaker back on and hurried upstairs to Janice's room. Taking a deep breath, he flipped the switch and the light came on! Geoff smiled broadly at his success.

"I'm proud of you!" Janice said to her husband as he showed her the working light. Geoff couldn't help but admit he was proud of himself.

***

A couple of days after Geoff had fixed Janice's ceiling light, she asked him a question that caught him off guard.

"Did you call Pastor Pete to thank him?"

Geoff's off–the-cuff response was, "No." After all, Pastor Pete hadn't actually helped him fix the light. Realizing how that sounded, he added, "I mean, I hadn't thought about calling him."

"Well Geoff, maybe you should."

Janice always had a way of stating things lovingly, but Geoff realized that while he considered it a suggestion, Janice meant for him to take it seriously.

"Okay," I'll give him a call on the way home from work tonight."

Later that morning, Geoff climbed into the Porsche and headed to the office. The day passed quickly, and before long he was back in the SUV, navigating the usual Pittsburgh traffic on his evening commute.

As he reached the outskirts of the city, he remember his promise to Janice and spoke the command aloud: "Call Pastor Pete." The car's system dialed the number, and soon the pastor's warm voice came through.

"Hello, Geoff!" Pastor Pete greeted him. After a bit of small talk, Geoff got to the point. "Hey, I wanted to thank you for your suggestions about the ceiling light. Turns out it was just a loose wire."

"I'm glad to hear it, Geoff. And at least you didn't have to buy a new light."

Almost by reflex, Geoff muttered, "Yeah, that's $149 that I can spend somewhere else."

There was a brief pause before Pastor Pete spoke again. "Is everything okay with you, Geoff?"

Now it was Geoff who struggled to find the words. "Well, truthfully, Pastor Pete, we've been having a bit of a hard time financially. We thought that when Janice went back to work a couple of years ago, our money problems would go away but they're still here."

"I'm sorry to hear that, Geoff," Pastor Pete said sympathetically. "I know you were at church this past Sunday. Did you know that we are holding a small group seminar on biblical financial practices?"

"Yeah, I heard about it," Geoff replied. "But I don't know if we can really commit the time." He hesitated. "Our lives are so busy…"

Pastor Pete gently countered, "I understand, Geoff. Life gets hectic. But I think it might benefit you and Janice to attend one of our groups. At least try it out for the first week?"

Geoff couldn't find the words to brush off the invitation. After thinking about it for a moment, he decided to inquire further.

"So, what exactly is the seminar about and what am I signing up for, Pastor?"

"We're going to discuss how people need to shift their focus from chasing material wealth and toward understanding what the bible teaches about money,

Pastor Pete explained. We believe that biblical financial teaching is sorely needed in our world today."

Geoff's memory drifted back to the previous service, and he spoke in a softer tone "Serving God with Money."

"Yes! Pastor Pete said, his tone brightening. "That's the title we're using for the seminar. We have already formed several small groups, but we still have slots for a few couples to join us."

"Couples?" Geoff asked, his voice tainted with surprise.

"Indeed." Pastor Pete confirmed, then added, "Since marriage is a partnership in all respects, we find it's critical that both husband and wife be a part of this process."

"Well, Pastor, I'll run this by Janice," Geoff replied, hoping she might halt the idea in its tracks.

Geoff bid Pastor Pete a good day and received a cheerful "God Bless you" in return as he hung up his cellphone using the steering wheel button.

Later that evening after dinner, the kids scattered to their rooms while Geoff and Janice loaded the dishwasher together. In the middle of their in small talk, Janice abruptly asked her husband "Oh, did you call Pastor Pete to thank him today?"

"Yes, I called him on my cell on the way home from the office, Geoff replied. He also invited us to join their small group seminar." Geoff chuckled through the last several words in an effort to lighten the subject.

But Janice was undeterred by his attempt at levity. "I think that's a wonderful idea, Geoff."

"You do?" he asked, perplexed by her enthusiasm.

"Yes, I do," Janice responded. "I've heard the announcement of this seminar at Church for weeks and was just waiting for the right moment to ask you about attending. I think it could help us understand our money issues."

Geoff was stunned, but he didn't want to let on.

"Well, if you want to go, I guess it's okay with me. But don't you think that the Church is just trying to get people to give more?"

"I think we should give it a try, Geoff," Janice said in that same soft tone that let him know she truly wanted him to accompany her to the seminar.

With the matter settled, Geoff immediately began to dread the arrival of Sunday morning.

CHAPTER

3

THE GROUP

The weekend was passing by quickly. Saturday was busy for the Wilson family. Kayla's soccer practice and Steven's baseball clinic were on the agenda, in addition to Janice's lunch with friends. Despite Geoff operating as the family taxi service, he managed to squeeze in nine holes with his buddies at Maple Crest golf Course.

As evening approached, the thought of Sunday morning started to weigh on Geoff's mind. "Janice, are we really going to this seminar tomorrow after Church?"

"Well, we did sign up and there's only three couples in the group", she reminded him. "It's going to be obvious if we're not there."

Geoff had to admit that their absence would be conspicuous, but then Janice provided a much stronger argument.

"In any case, I'm going, and I plan to apply what I learn at this seminar."

That was enough to settle Geoff's decision. He would attend the "Serving God with Money" seminar with his wife, even though he suspected it might just be a ploy by the Church to boost its contributions.

***

The next morning, Geoff dragged his feet as the time to leave for church approached. The rest of the family waited patiently downstairs, and when he heard the familiar call "Are you ready yet, Geoff?" he realized that it was time to stop procrastinating.

On his way out the door to the garage, Geoff doubled back to grab his trusty notebook and a pen. "This will show Janice that I'm 'invested' in this little seminar," he muttered to himself, a smirk crossing his face.

The family piled into the Porsche and arrived at the Church early enough to join their respective groups prior to worship. As the top of the hour arrived, the family regrouped and took their seats at the back of the sanctuary. The announcement scrolled across the large screens on opposite sides of the Cross, with frequent reminders that the "Serving God with Money" seminar would begin soon after the worship service ended.

It was another great message from Pastor Pete, who preached a sermon titled "Serving Multiple Masters" from **Matthew 6:19-24** as a preview of the upcoming seminar.

The congregation shuffled out of the sanctuary after worship. As the Wilson family exited, the kids congregated with their friends, as they were attending a companion seminar on the basics of finance.

Janice noticed that the LED screens in the atrium were directing attendees to assigned seminar rooms.

"It looks like we're in Room C, Geoff," Janice said, giving her husband a quick wave to direct him toward her.

As Geoff entered the room, he noticed most of the chairs were already taken. "Geoff!" Mike Bennett called out, standing and hurrying over to him. Extending his hand, he gave Geoff a vigorous handshake.

"Geoff and Janice, do you know my wife, Kathy?"

"Oh my, yes, we've met a few times!" Janice responded. Since he had not had the pleasure, Geoff introduced himself to Kathy with a smile. She smiled back and nodded warmly in return.

The other couple in the room were unfamiliar to Geoff. Seemingly more reserved, they were not ones to offer a greeting. But Janice, always the extrovert, broke the ice by introducing herself.

“I’m Janice, and this is my husband, Geoff.”

“I’m Tina,” the woman replied meekly.

“And I’m Fred Phillips,” the man added in a grumpy voice. He had his arms crossed on his chest as he quickly glanced up at Janice.

Geoff and Janice took two of the remaining seats around the table and briefly engaged in small talk until Pastor Pete entered Room C.

It was the time for the seminar to begin.

CHAPTER

4

THE SERVING GOD WITH MONEY MINDSET

"Welcome, everyone!" the Pastor exclaimed, greeting the group with a wide smile and open arms.

"Well, a big hello back to you!" yelled Mike in response, almost trying to outdo Pastor Pete's volume.

The seven people in the room exchanged introductions and settled in as seminar began.

"I would like to open with a moment of prayer," Pastor Pete said, bowing his head. The rest of the group followed suit.

"Heavenly Father, we pray that our time together today will be fruitful as we explore what Your Word teaches us about how we should think about money. Amen." Pastor Pete then raised his head and scanned the room to ensure that everyone was attentive and ready to begin.

"I'd like to begin by asking each of you what you hope to gain from our seminar. Mike, would you like to kick us off?"

"Sure, Pastor!" Mike replied exuberantly. Geoff couldn't help but glance at him wondering if there was an enthusiasm knob that could be turned down a little.

"Well, I'm looking forward to learning what the Bible says about money, and I'm hoping the harvest is plenty!"

Kathy spoke after Mike's statement. "I feel that we aren't doing enough to plan for our retirement or to support the Church. I'm hoping to find some answers to those questions."

Fred then joined the conversation. "We spend too much money. Or maybe I just don't make enough money since Tina doesn't work at all." Already shyly keeping her head down, Tina lowered it even further.

"Tina?" Pastor Pete prompted gently. "Would you like to go next?"

"I'm just here to learn," Tina said, her voice barely above a whisper.

"Ok then, Pastor Pete said with a smile. "Janice and Geoff, bring us home!"

"Well, Pastor," Janice began, "I went back to work at the bank so that our family could improve our financial situation. But after nearly two years, it doesn't appear that we have made any progress. In fact, I think our finances could be in worse shape than before I returned to work."

Geoff fidgeted in his chair, surprised and uncomfortable. It suddenly dawned on him that the same feelings he was experiencing had just been verbalized by his wife.

"And Geoff?" Pastor Pete prompted.

"What she said," Geoff curtly replied, pointing to Janice in the chair next to him.

Pastor Pete wrapped up the sharing time. "Great. So, let's begin by reading some Scripture together." He passed out the Bibles that were sitting on the table next to him so that everyone had their own.

"Now, please turn in your Bibles to the book of **Deuteronomy, chapter 8, verses 17 and 18**."

As each attendee opened their Bibles to the early books of the Old Testament, Mike was the first to find the passages. "May I read, Pastor Pete?" he asked.

A brief nod provided Mike with the confirmation to proceed.

Mike began, reading clearly, "*You may say to yourself, 'My power and the strength of my hands have produced this wealth for me.' But remember the Lord your God, for it is he who gives you the ability to produce wealth, and so confirms his covenant, which he swore to your ancestors, as it is today.*"

After a few moments, Pastor Pete continued.

"So, everything we earn in our careers all comes from God. And since He knows that our hearts follow what we treasure in this life –as we read in Matthew 6:21 – God wants to be first in our lives."

After a brief pause, Pastor Pete summarized the seminar in one phrase. "We have to make a choice. A choice between serving God or serving money, as we read in Matthew 6:24. I am suggesting that the way to choose God is to use our money to serve Him."

After a brief silence, Pastor Pete pushed back from the table. "But I'm getting a bit ahead of myself. Let's open our Bibles to the book of **Matthew, chapter 6.** We are going to read the passage that I preached on today."

As Pastor Pete scanned the room, his eyes met with Geoff, who quickly lowered his head.

"Geoff, would you please begin reading at verse 19? I'd then like each person to read one verse, ending at verse 24."

Geoff quickly turned the pages, scanning for the particular chapter that Pastor Pete had referenced. When he found Chapter 6, he began reading.

"*Do not store up for yourselves treasures on earth, where moths and vermin destroy, and where thieves break in and steal.*"

Janice continued at verse 20. "*But store up for yourselves treasures in heaven, where moths and vermin do not destroy, and where thieves do not break in and steal.*"

Tina, in a hushed voice, continued, "*For where your treasure is, there your heart will be also.*"

In a grumpy tone, Fred picked up at the next verse: "*The eye is the lamp of the body. If your eyes are healthy, your whole body will be full of light.*"

Kathy continued, "*But if your eyes are unhealthy, your whole body will be full of darkness. If then the light within you is darkness, how great is that darkness!*"

Mike's booming voice completed the reading. "*No one can serve two masters. Either you will hate the one and love the other, or you will be devoted to the one and despise the other. You cannot serve both God and money.*"

After Mike finished, the group sat in silence as they pondered on the end of verse 24.

CHAPTER

5

THE MINDSET IN ACTION

Pastor Pete thanked everyone for reading and then posed a follow-up question.

"What piques your interest in this passage?"

"Well, Pastor," Mike began, "It seems that some people place more importance on money than on God!"

"Yes, that's one conclusion that you could reach from Matthew's Gospel," Pastor Pete replied.

Geoff was surprised that Janice offered the next comment. "I was drawn to verse 19, where Jesus tells us not to store up treasures on earth."

"Interesting!" said Pastor Pete, leaning forward slightly. "Can you elaborate on that, Janice?"

"I think a lot of people in our community feel compelled to project a lifestyle that some may not be able to afford." The comment struck Geoff, and he realized that Janice might have been describing their family. He took the opportunity to jot this verse down in his notebook.

DO NOT STORE UP FOR YOURSELVES TREASURES ON EARTH

"Does anyone else agree with Janice's sentiment on verse 19?" Pastor Pete inquired.

There appeared to be tacit admission around the room that Janice's assessment was on point.

Pastor Pete then continued: "So, even though Jesus commands us to avoid doing so, why do many of us still feel the need to pursue the wealth of this world?"

"I guess we don't want to feel left out," Janice suggested.

"Or feel embarrassed that we don't have the best or the most expensive of everything," chimed in Kathy.

"The problem, as I see it, is that both spouses have to be on the same page!" Fred's frustration was coming through loud and clear.

"Indeed, marriage is a partnership on so many levels, but financial management is critical, Pastor Pete replied. What other lessons can we draw from Christ's words?" Pastor Pete asked, inviting others to speak.

Geoff decided it was time to offer his own insight. "It seems like verse 20 is just the opposite of the prior verse."

"Good point, Geoff!" Pastor Pete replied. "In the Bible, we find many contrasts such as verses 19 and 20. Christ commands us not to store up worldly treasures but rather treasures in heaven."

"How do we do that Pastor Pete?" Mike questioned.

"I think the passage provides us with guidance, Mike. Our hearts and our eyes will be focused on the treasures that we desire. We have to understand how to be focused on heavenly pursuits and how our money can assist in serving God."

"I'm confused, Pastor." Everyone in the room turned toward Tina, who had raised her head. "I think we all would admit that we're here because we are struggling with money. But we can't ignore the pursuit of money, can we? How would we survive?"

"Yes, and what about the saying that money is the root of all evil?" added Fred, piling on to the objection.

"Both great questions!" Pastor Pete responded. Instructing the group, he said, "Let's turn our Bibles to **First Timothy, Chapter 6**." Pastor Pete paused for a few moments as the group furiously flipped through the pages of the New Testament.

"And Fred, since you raised this question, would you please read for us verses 7-10?"

"Ok." Fred replied and then began reading. "For we brought nothing into the world, and we can take nothing out of it."

"But if we have food and clothing, we will be content with that. Those who want to get rich fall into temptation and a trap and into many foolish and harmful desires that plunge people into ruin and destruction."

"For the love of money is a root of all kinds of evil. Some people, eager for money, have wandered from the faith and pierced themselves with many griefs."

When Fred finished, he uttered one word. "Huh."

Pastor Pete prompted him with a follow-up question. "What did you find, Fred?"

"Well, I didn't realize that the Bible actually says that it is the love of money that is the root of all evil."

"Exactly!" said Pastor Pete excitedly. "You've uncovered the key word there, Fred. And it ties into what we've talked about in Matthew, chapter six."

"How so?" queried Geoff, genuinely interested in understanding the connection.

"Well, Geoff," Pastor Pete began, Matthew chapter six discusses where our treasures are, and how our hearts and eyes see that treasure. If you treasure something, Geoff, how does it make you feel?"

"I guess my feeling towards my treasure is…" Geoff paused, "Love?"

"Precisely!" Pastor Pete replied. "That is exactly what Paul writes to his protégé in chapter 6, verse 10 of his letter to Timothy. "He is essentially stating that if you love money, then money becomes your master."

Geoff picked up his pen and opened his notebook again, writing down the First Timothy verse (and underlining the word "love"):

THE LOVE OF MONEY IS THE ROOT OF ALL EVIL

"So, if the Bible tells us not to love money, why are we always trying to get more of it?" Janice questioned herself aloud.

After a few seconds of silence, Fred answered "That's the way the world works, isn't it, Pastor Pete?"

Pastor Pete smiled. "Fred, you've set me up again!" Let's turn our Bibles to Romans, chapter twelve to follow up on Fred's excellent point."

The group again furiously turned pages, with Tina arriving at the selected chapter of Romans first. "What verses are we reading, Pastor Pete?"

"Just the first half of verse 2, Tina."

With a now bolder voice, Tina read the verse. Concurrently with her reading it, Geoff again copied the Romans 12:2 verse into his notebook:

DO NOT BE CONFORMED TO THE WAYS OF THIS WORLD, BUT BE TRANSFORMED BY THE RENEWAL OF YOUR MIND.

After giving everyone a little time to ponder this verse, Pastor Pete put the question to the entire group.

"So, how does this verse respond to Fred's statement that the world is constantly pursuing money?"

"Well…" Mike began, then stopped when Kathy looked at him as if she wanted the opportunity to speak. "I was going to say that this verse is telling me that we need to be different than the world." Kathy gave her husband a brief smile.

"Yes, indeed!" Pastor Pete affirmed. "And it's the same with money as it is with a lot of other things in this world. We need to be a holy nation, a people set apart, as it is written in the letter of 1 Peter. We must think differently about money, recognizing that money is a tool, and what truly matters is how we respond to money, how we use money, and how we think about money, these choices determine whether we are using money to serve God."

"What does that look like when we apply this verse to our lives?" Geoff asked.

Pastor Pete smiled and scanned the room, turning his head, first to his left and then to his right.

"Ah, yes. The application of this verse can mean different things to different people. But it all leads back to Matthew chapter 6, particularly verse 21. Let me read that verse again for everyone."

Pastor Pete paused as he searched for the passage in his Bible.

"**For where your treasure is, your heart will be also**. Let's think about this verse before our next session together."

The group sat in silence, pondering on this thought as Pastor Pete closed the gathering with a prayer. The group rose from their chairs and exchanged their pleasant goodbyes to the other couples and to Pastor Pete. Geoff and Janice filed out of the room and drove home, each deep in thought, reflecting on the question: "Where are our hearts right now?"

CHAPTER

6

THE CONVERSATION

The following week flew by quickly, with both work and kids' schedules keeping the Wilson household busy. Janice attended a two-day offsite banking seminar mid-week, while Geoff filled the role of chauffeur, getting Kayla and Steven to various sports and music practices.

By the time the weekend arrived, the entire family was looking for some peace and quiet. However, Janice spoiled Geoff's Saturday plans by reminding him of their "homework assignment".

"Geoff, we need to spend some time discussing the verse from Matthew 6 before next Sunday," She said.

"We will, but I'm getting in nine holes at Maple Crest Golf Course this morning, Geoff said. Let's talk about it this afternoon."

Although the weather in Pittsburgh was unseasonably warm, it was not a great morning for Geoff. He shot a 42, several strokes above par and well above his usual average. He decided that Janice's insistence regarding Pastor Pete's assignment distracted him. Indeed, his mind was preoccupied with the question of where his heart truly lay regarding his treasure. By the time he returned home, he was ready for their conversation.

After lunch, Geoff and Janice settled into the morning room. The kids were in their respective bedrooms, and so they had the opportunity to talk without distractions.

"Do you want to start?" Geoff offered.

"I would prefer if you went first," Janice countered, and then added "You might not be thinking about this the same way that I am."

"Ok," Geoff responded, resigned to starting the conversation. "I think this passage is telling us to pursue wealth responsibly. While some people might lie, cheat or steal to get what they want, we are to do things the right way."

Janice nodded thoughtfully. "I agree with what you're saying, Geoff, but I think there's more here than doing things the right way."

"How so?" Geoff inquired.

"Well, there's a general attitude in this world, especially in our country, about money. Everyone wants it, desires it, and can't seem to get enough of it. It has become the master of many people, just as Pastor Pete mentioned."

"Go on" Geoff remarked, encouraging his wife to continue.

"I think we are to focus our hearts on things apart from the world," Janice added. The title of this seminar is 'Serving God with Money'. What if every Christian considered what God would want us to do before they made any major purchase? What if every Christian gave to the ministry of the Gospel without concern for the money they give?"

"Hmm, that's an interesting interpretation," Geoff responded. "But I'm not sure that's what this verse is telling me. It makes me feel like I shouldn't want nice things, that God frowns upon us spending money the way we do."

Janice stared at her husband, and Geoff could tell immediately that she did not agree with his perspective.

"But I'm sure we will hear more at our next session" Geoff quipped, hoping to keep his comment from starting an argument.

"Yes, our next meeting should be very…" Janice paused, sighed, and added, "Enlightening."

As the Wilsons and the Bennetts gathered after worship, it was apparent that the group was missing two people - Fred and Tina were not at Church and did not arrive at the seminar meeting room.

Pastor Pete entered the room after he finished greeting everyone after worship and noticed the puzzled looks around the meeting table. Preemptively answering the question apparent on their minds, he first let out a sigh.

"Fred and Tina Phillips will not be joining us today."

"Is anything wrong?" Kathy asked, her voice tinged with worry.

"I really can't speak to the reason behind their absence," Pastor Pete replied. "Now, let's get started!" He was obviously trying to change the subject and re-focus the conversation.

"I'm VERY interested to hear about your conversations regarding Romans 12:2 and how it speaks to Matthew 6:21!" Pastor Pete kicked off the conversation.

"Well, Pastor Pete!" Mike began in a booming voice, "Kathy and I had a great talk, and we agreed that our hearts should be in the right place."

"OK," Pastor Pete responded, "And where might that place be, Mike?"

"That's really all we discussed about the passage, Pastor."

With a look of slight disappointment on his face, Pastor Pete turned his body and his attention toward Geoff and Janice. As he folded his hands on top of the table, he asked "What did the two of you discuss?"

"Well, we didn't really agree on what the passage meant to us," Geoff admitted.

"Great!" was Pastor Pete's surprising response. He then asked them a follow-up question: "Where did the two of you differ on this verse?"

Geoff and Janice proceeded to recount their conversation from the night before, and Pastor Pete seemed quite impressed with their discussion about the treasure that their hearts were pursuing.

"So, let's talk about Geoff and Janice's conversation. I'd like to begin with the phrase 'set apart' from Romans 12:2 and what that really means."

"Does that mean we should not engage with people who don't think the way we do?" Kathy inquired.

"Not at all," Pastor Pete replied. "We are not set apart physically. In fact, there are many reasons why we don't want to be away from those who think differently than us."

"Then what does it mean to be set apart?" Geoff joined in on the line of questioning.

"Well, it means that our actions set us apart in a world that goes about its business differently."

"Hey, that's what we concluded!" Mike responded triumphantly.

"Yes," Pastor Pete reassured him. "But as Janice pointed out, practically it should focus our attention on everything that we do, even how we serve God with our money. And our hearts will follow the treasure that we pursue."

Geoff made a note to capture these points:

WE SHOULD BE SET APART FROM THE WORLD BY THE ACTIONS WE TAKE, EVEN WITH HOW WE USE OUR MONEY.

OUR HEARTS WILL FOLLOW THE TREASURE THAT WE PURSUE

The conversation continued around these two verses for some time. Mike and Geoff seemed like kindred spirits, as both were at odds with Janice and Kathy regarding the idea of being 'set apart'.

"I'm not saying that we shouldn't spend money or have nice things, dear," Janice reassured her husband.

"But spending just to keep up with, or outdoing, our neighbors doesn't seem prudent. Our hearts are in the wrong place if we do."

"It also doesn't allow us to Serve God with our money," Kathy pointed out, addressing both her husband and Geoff.

Pastor Pete then intervened, nodding toward the two ladies in the room. "I agree with their points, but recognize that yes, we are to enjoy God's blessings in our lives. This includes our money." Geoff folded his arms and leaned back in his chair, feeling validated by Pastor Pete's point.

"But there are questions that I ask myself before making any major purchase, and we will cover these in our discussion of Biblical spending."

As the session drew to a close, Pastor Pete closed the meeting with a prayer, and everyone agreed to reconvene again the following Sunday after Church.

CHAPTER

7

TOGETHER AGAIN

That next Sunday after worship, Geoff and Janice left the sanctuary and started walking down the hall to their "Serving God with Money" meeting room. They were both surprised when they noticed that Fred and Tina were entering the room ahead of them.

Even before they reached the room, they could hear Mike's voice greeting the returning couple that had missed the prior week. "Welcome back, you two!"

Geoff noticed as he entered the room that Fred seemed more relaxed, while Tina was infused with a confidence that he had not seen before.

"We're good," Fred offered, with a faint but noticeable smile forming on his face.

The sound of clapping drew the attention of all three couples toward the door. "Well, good to see everyone again!" Pastor Pete greeted the group, rubbing his hands together. "Why don't we get started?"

"Before we do," Tina interrupted, "I wanted to say something. Fred and I are sorry that we missed last week, but we had to have a lot of conversation as a couple about our financial situation."

"That's right," Fred added. "After our meeting two weeks ago, we met with Pastor Pete. We realized that our marital issues are tied to finances, and we need to be committed to this seminar."

"And we agreed that we are equal partners in this discussion," Tina interjected, as she reached for her husband's hand.

"Well, I for one am thrilled that you're back with us again!" Mike exclaimed.

"Yes, we're all happy to see you," Janice added warmly.

With that statement, Pastor Pete motioned everyone to take their seats so that the week's seminar could begin.

***

"To start today's session, I would like to begin by reading a few verses from **Luke, chapter 14**." Pastor Pete cleared his throat, opened his Bible, and began to read.

"For which of you, desiring to build a tower, does not first sit down and count the cost, whether he has enough to complete it? Otherwise, when he has laid a foundation and is not able to finish, all who see it begin to mock him, saying, 'This man began to build and was not able to finish.'"

He closed the Bible, folded his hands on the meeting room table and smiled, tilting his head back and forth. "Let me provide some context for this passage. Jesus is speaking to a large crowd about the cost of following him."

Pastor Pete paused and noted that everyone in the room were engaged before he continued. "Jesus then follows these verses by comparing the building of a tower to a king, who is deciding whether he should go into battle against another king."

After a few moments, Geoff broke the silence. "How does this apply to our financial situation Pastor?"

"You tell me," Pastor Pete replied.

"Well, the theme that jumps out at me is one of preparation." This response was surprisingly offered by Fred.

"Yes!" Pastor Pete confirmed, then asked a follow-up question. "What do both the builder and the king have in common?"

After a period of contemplation, Janice offered a suggestion. "I think both of them were taking a big risk as they began their endeavor, and they needed to assess whether they could succeed."

"That's great!" Pastor Pete responded. "Does anyone else have any other thoughts?"

"These scenarios in the Bible make me think that we need to have a plan for our money, or else we won't be able to achieve our financial goals."

The entire room turned their attention to Kathy, as the realization dawned upon the room.

"You got us, Pastor Pete!" Mike added with a wry smile. "We need to take the time to plan, and I will admit that Kathy and I don't do this very often."

"By 'very often', Mike means we don't do it at all." Kathy added, using air quotes to accentuate her point. She offered a chuckle to her comment as Mike glanced over at her.

"Look, not enough people take the opportunity to create a plan for their money," Pastor Pete assured the couples in the room. "Let me offer an example. Many of us are sports fans, yes? How much fun would it be to watch sports if there wasn't a scoring system?"

"I wouldn't watch at all!" Geoff admitted out loud.

"We wouldn't know who won," Fred added.

"Exactly. Then how can you win at finances if you don't track your success along the way?"

This example seemed to resonate with the group, as heads nodded in agreement.

Geoff opened his notebook and, with a pen in his hand, recorded two statements to capture this concept:

YOU MUST PREPARE TO BE FINANCIALLY SUCCESSFUL!

YOU CAN'T WIN IN FINANCES IF YOU DON'T TRACK YOUR SUCCESS ALONG THE WAY!

The group continued their discussion on the importance of preparation, and as they were about to depart, Pastor Pete assigned some homework.

"I want to give you an assignment for next week's session," he said, reaching into a folder and handing out a copy of a form titled 'Biblical Budgeting: Serving God with Money.'

For a copy of this Biblical Budgeting form, please visit our companion website:

www.ServingGodwithmoney.org

"I'm also going to email you this budgeting form as a

spreadsheet. It will allow you to enter your numbers, and the spreadsheet will calculate the totals automatically."

The couples reviewed the form and agreed to return the following week with their information completed.

Pastor Pete closed the Biblical Budgeting session with a prayer, and then everyone shared blessings for a good week before parting ways.

CHAPTER

8

BIBLICAL BUDGETING

"We need to schedule some time to fill out that Biblical Budgeting form before next Sunday!" Janice said firmly, and Geoff realized it was useless to resist. Letting out a deep sigh, he resigned himself to missing the following night's football game on TV. "Okay, he said. Let's sit down tomorrow night. The kids have too much going on this weekend, so tomorrow will be the best evening to get this done."

The following night, with their recent financial records gathered around them, Geoff and Janice meticulously filled out the form. The results were very surprising. In particular, the costs for vacation and car payments were particularly eye opening to the couple.

"We're in a negative budget situation!" Geoff announced with a surprised tone. "How did we not understand this before?"

"Because we never took the time and energy to calculate our income and expenses before," Janice responded. "That's why we are taking this seminar."

Geoff had no comeback to his wife's assessment.

As Sunday arrived, Janice gathered the completed form and called to Geoff, who was upstairs. "Let's get moving up there! We'll be late for Church!" Like a petulant child, Geoff grumpily descended the stairs and headed out to the garage.

The Church service was very uplifting, and as the congregation dispersed for their Sunday afternoon itineraries, the Wilsons turned left out of the Sanctuary and headed down to their meeting room, the other two couples had already assembled.

After greetings were exchanged, the group waited patiently as Pastor Pete welcomed the remaining Church attendees. Once he finished, he entered the room with a big smile on his face.

"How did things go with your assignment?" Pastor Pete queried as he took his seat.

It was apparent from the looks around the room that all three couples' eyes were opened by the results.

"We didn't realize how much we were spending in certain areas," Tina admitted.

"I think we better understand why we needed to participate in this seminar," Kathy added.

"Ok, it sounds like the results of your budgeting surprised you. That's why, as Kathy said, you're all here. Understanding how God wants us to serve Him through our financial blessings is our focus."

"So, what exactly does God want us to do with our money?" Mike questioned.

"Great query!" Pastor Pete responded enthusiastically. "It's really the perspective that we take with our money that is important. If we are to provide our 'first fruits' financially, we need to budget in this manner."

"How so?" Janice wondered aloud.

"First, let's consider how most people approach budgeting. That is, the people who take time to budget in the first place."

Pastor Pete reached into his file and distributed a one page summary to each of the six attendees around the table.

"On the left side is the traditional 'Money Stack', presented in the order of importance that most people use to construct their budgeting. It focuses first on the amount that families spend. The budget then moves to 'what is left over', if anything, so that saving and investing can occur. And finally, giving occurs if there is any remaining excess."

Geoff stared at the exhibit that Pastor Pete had handed out, realizing that his approach to budgeting in his head aligned closely with the traditional 'Money Stack" approach. He shared his thoughts with the group. "Eye opening, to say the least."

Traditional "Money Stack"	Biblical "Money Stack"
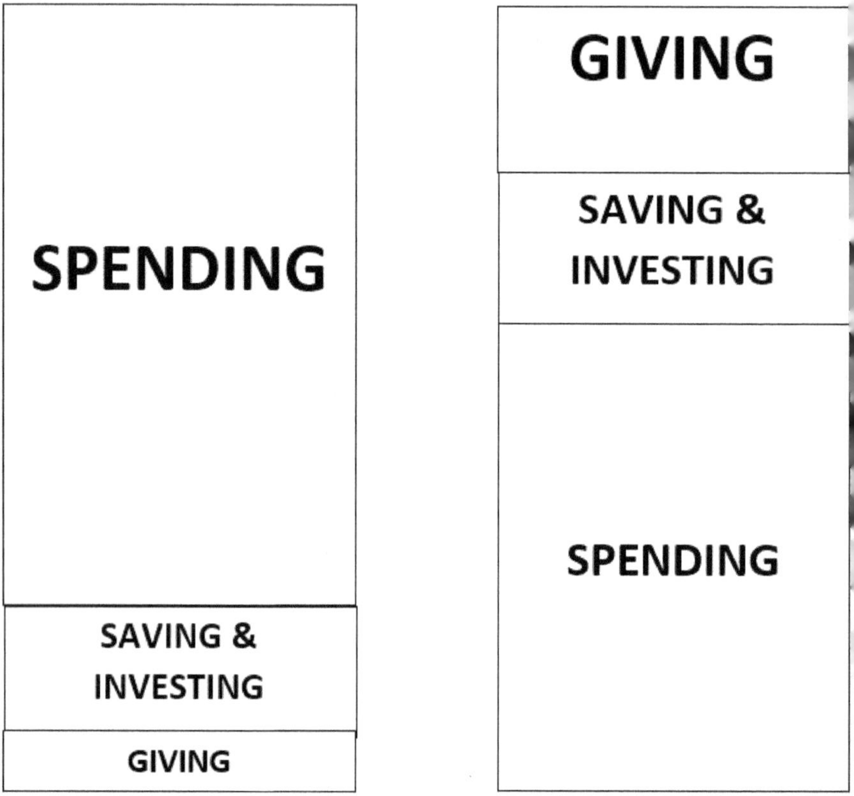 SPENDING	GIVING
SAVING & INVESTING	SAVING & INVESTING
GIVING	SPENDING

For a copy of this Money Stack exhibit, please visit our companion website:

www.ServingGodwithmoney.org

The others also seemed deep in thought, but none verbalized that they approached budgeting any differently than the traditional approach of their own 'Money Stack'.

Pastor Pete broke the silence. "Now, the approach on the right side shows how a biblical 'Money Stack' would be structured. And it ties back to this concept of 'first fruits,' where we essentially commit to paying God first."

"You see that the Biblical Money Stack is really the Traditional Money Stack flipped upside down, yes?"

After a few moments to let this idea sink in, Pastor Pete continued. "Our next step is to think about preserving some of our 'Money Stack' for the future. This concept can be summarized as 'paying ourselves next'. There are many Bible verses that discuss how we do so, by saving and investing in a prudent, Christian manner. But that will be for another day."

"And what's left is what we spend?" Fred asked.

"And in doing so, we put our spending on the bottom of the stack," Tina commented.

"Exactly!" Pastor Pete confirmed. "This is the concept of enjoying the fruits of our labor. God really does want us to enjoy our lives here on earth, and we will discuss this topic as well in a future session."

While the group paused to reflect upon this division of the Biblical Money Stack, Geoff wrote down these three concepts in his notebook:

PAY GOD FIRST

PAY OURSELVES NEXT

ENJOY THE FRUITS OF OUR LABOR

Drumming his pen on his notebook, Geoff stared at what he wrote with a slight amount of derision etched on his face. Janice reciprocated Geoff's frown with a look of disappointment.

"Pastor Pete, I'm wondering how often we should budget, every month?" Tina asked. Pastor Pete responded by shaking his head back and forth.

"Your annual budget should be prepared once a year, usually toward the end of the year as you adjust your previous year's budget for the following year."

Fred followed up his wife's question: "So, how do we track how we're doing?"

"You record your previous month's spending each month on another form!" Pastor Pete was almost giggling as he reached into his folder and distributed a form appropriately titled 'Monthly Spending Record'. It had a column for each month, and the left side of the form reflected the same categories as the budget form, albeit with a few open lines for custom budget items.

"You can track your progress as the year goes on, and if new categories are required, you will find a few blank lines to update the form with your custom spending."

"But Pastor Pete," Kathy began, "Shouldn't we budget for these 'custom' items?"

For a copy of this Monthly Spending Form, please visit our companion website:

www.ServingGodwithmoney.org

"Not for the full year, but you can update your budget for the following year if these 'custom' budget items will be recurring," Pastor Pete said. You could also assign a budgeted amount for the remaining months of the year if the costs are ongoing."

"Seems like a lot of work," Geoff mumbled under his breath. Unfortunately for him, Janice heard his remark and bowed her head while stretching out her folded hands. Geoff could not help but notice her displeasure.

With no further discussion for the week, Pastor Pete's prayed to close the meeting, and Geoff and Janice headed home. The Wilsons did not discuss their session, choosing instead to reflect on the content of their discussion and their conclusions.

CHAPTER

9

THE MOMENT OF TRUTH

While the following week was passing by rapidly, Geoff and Janice had not spoken about the previous "Serving God with Money" session. That Friday evening, after a dinner of carryout pizza, the kids retired to their rooms, giving their parents time to discuss the previous Sunday's session.

"Well, I for one really enjoyed last week's seminar," Janice began. She realized that her husband was less impressed. "You don't seem to share my reaction," she observed.

Geoff paused and sighed. "I'm still not quite sure how this is going to help us, Janice. It doesn't change that our 'money stack' is the same size, and I don't see how turning it upside down will help us with our money problems."

"That's fine, as long as you are willing to continue seeing this through to the end of the seminar. We can then both evaluate the impact on our financial lives." Geoff agreed with a slight nod and a faint smile, although he couldn't admit to Janice that he was considering dropping out of the seminar altogether.

As Sunday arrived, the Wilson family piled into their SUV for the drive to Church. Geoff's face clearly indicated his lack of interest, causing Janice to pat him on the shoulder. "We'll make it through today's meeting and talk if you want to continue." Geoff glanced over and smiled genuinely at the potential exodus opportunity.

After another great worship service and sermon from Pastor Pete, the couple turned left out of the Sanctuary. When they did, Mike and Kathy were standing there. "Can we talk?" Mike offered in a hushed tone, without his normal exuberance. Geoff confirmed with a nod and gestured to an open room near them.

The two couples sat down at the round table. Mike unsurprisingly began the conversation. "Kathy and I are not sure if we are going to continue with the seminar."

But Kathy immediately corrected him: "Wrong! I want to continue, but Mike isn't so sure."

"Geoff is having the exact same thoughts." Janice added, looking down a bit as she made the statement. "I've agreed that if he wants to quit after today's session, then we can do so."

"Why do you want to quit, Geoff?" Kathy inquired.

Now it was Geoff looking down at his shoes. "I'm not certain if we are getting a big benefit out of the seminar."

"Do you want to know what I think?" Janice interjected. "I think that both you and Mike are not happy to hear that we are having financial issues, and maybe you feel embarrassed?"

Geoff lifted his head and glared at her. But as he met her gaze, he had to make the admission that had been on his mind. "I think you're right, honey. After our budgeting exercise, I realized that I am not providing for the family as I should."

"Oh, dear," Janice responded, extending her palms to grasp her husband's hands. "I don't feel that way at all. We're doing well when it comes to earning our money. We're just not taking the appropriate actions to manage our finances. That's why we're here, attending this seminar. I think if we apply what we're learning in this seminar, it will help us financially. Please, let's see it through."

Geoff pondered on Janice's heartfelt comments. After a few moments, he smiled and offered a simple reply: "Ok. I'm on board."

"Me too!" Mike responded, his characteristic enthusiasm shining through. Together, the two couples left the room to meet the others for that week's seminar session.

CHAPTER

10

BIBLICAL BUDGETING IN ACTION

The Wilsons and the Bennetts made their way to the seminar room, where both Fred and Tina as well as Pastor Pete were waiting for them.

"Please, sit down folks." Pastor Pete offered the invitation as he extended his hands outward.

"Last week, we talked about the 'Biblical Money Stack' and the three essential concepts. Can anyone recall those three concepts?"

Geoff jumped in before the others. "Yes, the concepts are pay God first, pay ourselves next and enjoy the fruits of our labor." He couldn't hide the self-satisfied look on his face. Janice also seemed proud of Geoff's engagement level.

"Excellent, Geoff. Now, I'm going to ask each of you to get out your Biblical Budgeting forms and let's analyze each of these three categories together.

As each of the couples retrieved the form from their respective folders, Pastor Pete passed out another form, which listed each of the three categories that Geoff had just recited. Next to the categories was a space for writing the amounts from the budget form. The title of this form read "Biblical Budgeting Allocation Form".

For a copy of this Biblical Budgeting Allocation Form, please visit our companion website:

www.ServingGodwithmoney.org

"I want you to write your dollar figures from your Biblical Budgeting form for each of the three categories on this paper I've handed out."

Pastor Pete held up his phone. "Then, using the calculator on your phone, let's tally the percentages of each category."

The couples spent the next few minutes performing the calculations. After confirming that each couple was finished, Pastor Pete then asked,

"Does anyone feel like sharing? This is a safe space to share these percentages."

"We will." Janice surprised Geoff with her offer. Pastor Pete motioned for Janice to proceed.

"Pay God First percentage - 2%, Pay Ourselves Next - 5%, and Enjoy the fruits of our labor - 93%."

The room fell silent when Janice finished. Pastor Pete smiled and reassured everyone "Thank you so much for sharing, Janice." He paused before continuing, "Fred and Tina?"

"Our percentages were similar to Janice and Geoff's numbers: 3%, 3%, and 94%.

Kathy proactively offered their percentages: "2%, 2% and 96%."

"What are your first impressions?" Pastor Pete inquired.

"My impression is that we are spending a lot of our 'money stack' if you will," Geoff observed. "But I really don't see how flipping the stack is going to change anything."

"I understand your skepticism, Geoff. May I ask you a question?"

"Of course," Geoff responded.

"If something comes up that you're not expecting, how do you deal with that situation from a financial perspective?" The room turned their focus to Geoff as they awaited his response.

"Well, I guess we use our credit cards or home equity line of credit when something arises that we didn't expect."

Pastor Pete folded his hands in front of his mouth, letting his silence linger for a little while. "So, approximately how much are you paying as interest on those two debt options? And keep in mind, we are talking specifically about using debt.

"I'd have to check, Pastor," Geoff answered. "It's been a while since I looked at that information."

"According to a recent report, the average credit card interest rate is over 24%,"[1] Pastor Pete reported to the group. That statement was met with stunned silence.

"That means that in just over three years, using credit cards today for any purchase will double the cost of that purchase."

Geoff fumbled with his pen. "I'm not sure how in today's world we can live without utilizing debt."

---

[1] "Average Credit Card Interest Rate for March 2025", Investopedia.

Pastor Pete looked down, as if to sympathize with Geoff. "I understand. This world tells us to pursue our financial dreams and not to worry about the costs."

He continued with his counterargument: "This is what **Romans 12:2** instructs. We shouldn't be conformed to the ways of this world. But we CAN renew our minds if we budget from a biblical perspective."

"I'm certainly curious!" The traditionally enthusiastic Mike proclaimed.

"Great!" Pastor Pete replied. "Then let's get started. While addressing our debt is critical, the first thing that you need is a plan for any financial emergencies.

The group gave Pastor Pete their full attention.

Pastor Pete took a breath and explained: "It may sound counterintuitive, but the first thing that you need to do is create a savings account."

"Rather than paying down debt?" Janice questioned the Pastor.

"Yes, but the good news is it shouldn't take too long if you are willing to make sacrifices. But first, let's turn our Bibles to **Matthew chapter 25**. Who would like to read the first 13 verses of that chapter for everyone?"

"I'll volunteer," said Fred, who already had his Bible open and was very close to reading the passage.

Once he found the start of chapter 25 in the Gospel of Matthew, he read:

“[1]At that time, the kingdom of heaven will be
like ten virgins who took their lamps and went out to
meet the bridegroom. [2]Five of them were foolish and
five were wise. [3]The foolish ones took their lamps but
did not take any oil with them. [4]The wise ones,
however, took oil in jars along with their lamps. [5]The
bridegroom was a long time in coming, and they all
became drowsy and fell asleep.

[6]“At midnight, the cry rang out: ‘Here’s the
bridegroom! Come out to meet him!’

[7]“Then all the virgins woke up and trimmed their
lamps. [8]The foolish ones said to the wise, ‘Give us
some of your oil; our lamps are going out.’

[9]‘No,’ they replied, ‘there may not be enough for
both us and you. Instead, go to those who sell oil and
buy some for yourselves.’

[10]“But while they were on their way to buy the oil,
the bridegroom arrived. The virgins who were ready
went in with him to the wedding banquet. And the
door was shut.”

[11]“Later the others also came. ‘Lord, Lord,’ they
said, open the door for us!”

[12]“But he replied, ‘Truly, I tell you, I don’t know
you.”

13 "Therefore, keep watch because you do not know the day or the hour."

When Fred finished, he closed his Bible and raised his head.

Pastor Pete queried the room "What word would you use to describe the five virgins who had to go back to get their oil?"

After a few moments of contemplation, Tina provided a response: "Irresponsible is the word I'd choose."

The group agreed that this word offered the best description.

Pastor Pete verbalized in his preacher's voice: "The biblical meaning of this passage refers to those who are not prepared for Jesus to return. But there is an application to our financial situation. Five of the women were ready when the groom arrived, the other five were not and wasted precious time."

Geoff interrupted: "I'm not following, Pastor Pete."

"What if ten people are facing the same immediate financial need, such as the groom arrived at midnight in the parable? All ten ladies knew the groom could come at some point, just as we all know that a financial emergency occurs in each of our own lives. What if only five of those people were responsible and had an

'Ark Account' while the other five were, as Tina stated, irresponsible?"

The couples around the table thought about that perspective.

Janice broke the silence. "So, you're suggesting, Pastor Pete, that we should be responsible enough to have savings, right?"

"Not just savings," Pastor Pete responded. "But separate savings designed and earmarked to meet a financial need that arrives that you're not expecting. Much like the five of the women did not have any oil when the groom arrived."

"Savings that are separated from other savings?" Mike asked the financial question that others might have been considering.

"Yes, it's best if these savings are in separate accounts and accessed only when an unplanned need arrives. The car breaks down. The furnace needs replaced. Or if a catastrophic event occurs, such as one where you lose your income."

"You mean fired, Pastor?" Fred replied. Pastor Pete nodded.

"Some people call it an 'Emergency Fund' or a 'Rainy Day' account. In the spirit of Noah, I've come to call it the 'Ark Account'."

A Fund that could be used for your own," Pastor Pete paused for effect. "Or others' needs."

"Wait, so now I'm saving for not just the Wilsons but for the Bennetts too?" Geoff shouted and threw his hands in the air in a joking fashion. But for Geoff, there was a kernel of a question that he was trying to affirm.

"Well, yes, Geoff," Pastor Pete answered. "For anyone that you know that might have a financial hardship, when you have reached the point where you want to 'Serve God with Money', you need to be prepared to help those who are not prepared. For those who might be, well, irresponsible."

Mike raised an eyebrow and looked sideways at Pastor Pete.

"I'm not specifically singling YOU out Mike." Pete responded and received a hearty amount of laughter around the room, including from Mike himself.

Tina stopped the laughter with a serious question: "But, if we're all struggling with finances right now, then how are we supposed to start this 'Ark Account'. And how much should be in this 'Account' to know that we're good to go?"

Kathy followed up Tina's questions with one of her own: "Oh, and what happens when we actually use the money in this Fund for an unplanned financial need?"

"Great questions, and ones that we will tackle in our next session." Pastor Pete then closed the seminar session with a prayer and bid the couples a good Sunday afternoon.

CHAPTER

11

BUILDING AN 'ARK ACCOUNT'

The following week was another busy one for the Wilson family. As the weekend arrived, Geoff found himself anticipating the next 'Serving God with Money' seminar meeting, possibly for the first time. Janice noticed Geoff's changed demeanor, and he was ready to leave for Church before she was on Sunday morning.

Another great time of worship together ended, and immediately the energized triumvirate of couples made their way to the seminar room. The couples were engaging in small talk when Pastor Pete entered the room with a wide smile on his face.

"Well, it looks like we've got a noisy group today!" Pastor Pete observed. "So, let's get started by reviewing the questions that were raised at the end of last week's session."

The group settled in, and Geoff readied his pen hovering above his notebook.

"My recollection is that the following questions were asked as our time together last week ended:

- How are we supposed to start this 'Ark Account'?
- How much should be in this 'Fund' to know that we're good to go?
- What happens when we actually use the money in this Fund for an unplanned financial need?"

Pastor Pete attempted to calm any anxiety in the room: "These are great questions, and many couples struggle with establishing an Ark Account. A recent survey found that 62% of Americans don't believe they have enough emergency savings, while only 20% increased their savings last year."[2]

He continued. "The first question is how to start this Ark Account. The best way to do this is to open a separate account with your banking institution that is to be used solely for financial reserves."

"You can't use an existing account?" Mike inquired.

---

[2] Bankrate.com Survey by Karen Bennett, October 23, 2024.

"You could, but then you're mixing what is reserve money with funds you use for paying bills, buying necessities, and other items." Pastor Pete replied.

"And that could get confusing because you might compromise your reserves for luxury purchases if you do so."

"I agree with you Pastor Pete. It should be a separate account," Kathy stated plainly as she glanced toward her husband.

"Once we establish this 'Ark Account', how do we save enough for a financial emergency?" Fred asked. "And how much is 'enough' to have in this Ark Account?"

Responding to Fred's second question, Pastor Pete said, "How much is enough will be up to each of you, but even just one month of after-tax salary is a great place to begin. More is better."

"But if we're having financial issues, how do we save that much money?" Geoff asked.

"Good question. Let's brainstorm some ways to build up this Ark Account."

Janice began by offering an option: "Well, selling something that you no longer use would be one way."

"Great idea!" Pastor Pete exclaimed. "Other thoughts?"

"Maybe take fewer vacations each year? Or shorter vacations? Or less expensive vacations?" Kathy queried, obviously focused on the vacation topic. She and Mike exchanged glances after she verbalized her suggestion.

"Yes! Again, a small sacrifice that can end up funding your emergency fund all at once!"

"How about not eating out or ordering food and cooking more at home?" Geoff smiled after making this suggestion.

"Or attending fewer Steelers, Penguins or Pirates games" Janice added as Geoff scowled.

"All good ideas, and all involve a small sacrifice that can go a long way to getting your Ark Account to a level that allows you to begin to tackle your debt. But you have to be deliberate about placing those savings into your Ark Account."

"But when would we use the money in the Ark Account and what do we do once we use it?" Tina asked.

"Well, Tina, you use the money whenever an emergency arises in place of using debt, and you then immediately turn your attention to rebuilding your Ark Account."

"So," Geoff asked, "it's up to us?"

"Of course!" Pastor Pete replied.

Geoff took out his pen and wrote the responses to the three questions:

- How are we supposed to start this 'Ark Account'? ***Selling something you no longer use, taking fewer vacations, cooking more at home, attending fewer sporting events, etc.***
- How much should be in this Fund to know that we're good to go? ***One month after-tax salary is a good start, more is better.***
- What happens when we actually use the money in this Fund for an unplanned financial need?" ***Immediately turn our attention to rebuilding the Ark Account.***

"I can see how important it is to have an Ark Account for financial emergencies," Janice stated. "But how do we deal with the debt that we've already accumulated? It isn't going away while we're building up the Ark Account."

"That's what we will discuss next week!" Pastor Pete responded. As he gathered his papers, the three couples got up from the table to leave. But before they could walk out of the room, Pastor Pete stopped them.

"Oh, and one more item for next week: please bring information on all of your debts, the balance, minimum payment and interest rate for each debt, to our next session." He then closed the session with prayer.

CHAPTER

12

SMASHING DOWN YOUR DEBT STACK

The following week, an eager group of couples arrived after worship in their "Serving God with Money" seminar meeting room.

Pastor Pete entered the room, quickly greeted everyone, opened with prayer and began the week's seminar, picking up on the prior week's Debt introduction.

"Just as there is the Money Stack, there is also the Debt Stack. I hope all of you brought your debt information as I requested." As he said this, Pastor Pete handed out another piece of paper to each couple from his folder.

"I would like you to analyze your debts by ranking your loans from highest to lowest amounts and then noting the associated minimum payment and interest rate with each item of debt."

Geoff smiled as he received the handout from Pastor Pete. He quickly noticed the title "Smashing Down Your Debt Stack" at the top and had three columns. One column was labeled 'Amount', the second 'Minimum Payment', and the third 'Interest Rate'.

The 'Amount' and 'Minimum Payment' columns also had a total line at the bottom of the list.

For a copy of this Smashing Down Your Debt Stack Form, please visit our companion website:

www.ServingGodwithmoney.org

The couples quickly understood the exercise and quickly got to work on completing the form. Geoff and Janice partnered together, sorting their various debts as described in the exercise while the other couples did the same.

"Given the information that you have just completed, can you see how much your ability to Pay God First and Pay Yourself Next is undermined by your debt?" Pastor Pete paused again to let that statement sink in, as it was apparent that the couples were responsible for building an unenviable list of debts.

Pastor Pete sat back in his chair and scanned the faces of the couples in the room. "Do you remember the story in Exodus chapter 4? That chapter begins with Moses doubting his ability to make the people listen to the Word of God. But then God asks him in verse 2: 'What is that in your hand?' Do any of you recall what Moses held in his hand?"

"Yes, a staff," Janice replied.

"Indeed! Something that Moses already possessed. Something that he was familiar with using and used regularly. How does this apply to our discussion of debt?"

"I think I know!" Tina chimed in. "When we use credit cards and other forms of debt, we are reaching for something not already in our hands."

"Yes!" Pastor Pete confirmed. "And we must ask ourselves whether God intends for us to reach for things He has not blessed us to receive at that time."

He paused. "Look, since I expect you to be honest with me, I should also be honest with you. In my younger days, I got into some trouble with credit card debt. I was approved for several credit cards in my late teens and early 20's, accepted those invitations to pile on debt, and eventually had to get rid of them so that

I wouldn't continue to abuse debt anymore. I had to really buckle down on my spending to generate the funds to pay off those credit cards. It was very difficult."

As he surveyed the eyes of the people around the table, Pastor Pete could see that this admission surprised them.

Sighing deeply, he continued, "It's one of the reasons that I started these 'Serving God with Money' seminars. Many Christians do not manage their financial situation using biblical principles. They let their Debt Stack dominate how they use their Money Stack. We hope that we can begin to change that here at Living Water Church."

Geoff shook his head and chuckled, catching everyone's attention. "And here I thought you were just lecturing us, Pastor Pete. I didn't realize that you have had a similar experience. Thank you, thank you for opening up and being honest with us. It's very refreshing."

The remainder of the group nodded to confirm their appreciation of Pastor Pete's personal story.

"Thanks, everyone," Pastor Pete stated humbly. "This is why it is so important to Smash Down your Debt Stack, pay off your debts and make that stack flatter than a pancake." Pastor Pete emphasized this point with a visual demonstration, pushing both hands on top of a theoretical Debt Stack to the table. This action prompted smiles and a few chuckles around the table.

"It will allow you to implement the Biblical Money Stack and bring a sense of calm to your finances that will allow you to live a Christian financial life."

"So, how exactly should we 'Smash Down' our Debt Stack?" Mike inquired, "I mean, we aren't going to be able to make more money than we already earn."

"Most people don't have an earnings problem, Geoff. They have a spending and debt problem." Geoff nodded voluntarily, even though he wasn't entirely sure he agreed with Pastor Pete.

"That's why I asked you to rank your debts, from the smallest to largest by amount. If you think of the debt stack as a pyramid, with your smallest debt at the top, you're using a method that will help you in 'smashing down your debt stack.'

"I'm intrigued!" Mike declared. "Can you explain to us how 'smashing down your debt stack' actually works?"

"You make the minimum payment on all of your debts except your smallest one. You focus all of your remaining debt repayment budget on your smallest debt until it's paid off."

"Why wouldn't we focus on paying off the debt with the highest interest rate?" Janice questioned.

"Ah yes," Pastor Pete replied, "while that method would provide the biggest relief for your interest payments, a 2016 study by the Harvard Business Review found it didn't work effectively as 'smashing down your debt stack'".

"That's a surprising discovery," Kathy responded, while the others nodded in agreement and then asked a follow up question. "Why is that the case, Pastor Pete?"

"Their research indicated that people were more motivated to get out of debt if they began with their smallest amount.

This method provided them with a sense of progress as they saw the number of total debts they had reduced."[3]

"And they termed it 'Smashing Down your Debt Stack'?" Geoff inquired.

"No, that phrase is one of my invention!" Pastor Pete proudly proclaimed. He again motioned with his hands pressing down toward the table, eliciting smiles around the room.

---

[3] Harvard Business Review, "Research: The Best Strategy for Paying Off Credit Card Debt" by Remi Trudel

"But how do we effectively budget for paying our debt, Pastor Pete?" This time it was Mike who had asked the question.

"You should find a way to budget as much as you can, Mike," Pastor Pete said. "If you look at your Debt Stack page, you have totaled your minimum payment at the bottom of that column. You should strive to target a budget of at least twice that amount for your debt repayments each month, but more would be better of course."

Pastor Pete paused for a moment before continuing. "And another thing, you have to STOP using your debt immediately. No more credit card usage, no more drawing on a home equity line of credit. The only way you can 'smash down your debt stack' is to effectively 'cut yourselves off' from debt." Pastor Pete used air quotes for emphasis on the phrase 'cut yourselves off.'

"But what if an emergency happens?" Geoff offered but then caught himself. "Oh, I almost forgot. When that happens, we use our Ark Account."

"Correct," Pastor Pete acknowledged. "That's why you create the Ark Account first before 'Smashing Down your Debt Stack.'"

"How long will it take to 'Smash our Debt Stack' down to nothing, Pastor Pete?

"Of course, the answer, Janice, is that it depends. It depends on the size of your Debt Stack, the interest rates of each debt, and the extra amount over the minimum payments that you commit to 'Smashing' your Debt."

"Wow, we've lived with our debt for a long time!" Fred declared, raising his eyebrows as a grin formed across his face. "I'm sure going to miss it."

Fred's comment elicited laughter around the room, but there was a sense of lightness at the thought of being free from debt.

"Well, don't get too comfortable," Pastor Pete warned. "At our seminar next week, we will discuss biblical principles that should guide and govern our spending." He then closed the session with prayer and wished the couples a productive week before they gathered again.

CHAPTER

13

BIBLICAL SPENDING

As the following week passed, Geoff and Janice found a quiet moment one evening to discuss what they had learned. Janice seemed surprised when Geoff proactively broached the subject.

"I think we should talk about last week's seminar. I am glad that we signed up for 'Serving God with Money'. And I think we should take some time to identify a few ways that we can save some money and start an Ark Account."

Janice was noticeably pleased and walked into the kitchen to grab a notepad and a pen. "Sounds, great honey!" she said.

The Wilsons sat at the kitchen table and over the next hour, they worked out a plan to create their Ark Account. They debated and agreed on one big idea that would allow them to get the Ark Account on track quickly.

Geoff felt a great deal of satisfaction at their progress and stopped by the bank later in the week to open the new account for the Ark Account.

As Sunday morning arrived, Geoff and Janice urged Kayla and Steven to get ready for worship. As they hopped into their Porsche, the Wilson parents glanced over at each other. Janice then turned around to the back seat and informed the children of some decisions that they had made.

"Kids, we're going to be trading in this car for one that will cut our payments in half."

Both of the Wilson children looked surprised, but Janice's next statement had a greater impact on them.

"And we will be taking only one vacation in the Spring."

While Kayla and Steven let that thought sink in, Geoff pulled into the Living Water Church parking lot to drop off the family. As he pulled away from the entrance area to the Church, he noticed that many cars in the lot were expensive imports, and wondered aloud "How many of these folks are in our 'Serving God with Money' seminars right now?" He parked the car, entered the Church and headed toward the sanctuary.

After an inspirational worship service, the couples gathered in their regular meeting room. Moments after everyone was seated, Pastor Pete entered with a big smile on his face.

"Are we ready for our topic today?" Heads nodded in general agreement, but Geoff was still bracing for impact. He had been worrying all week about this discussion of spending but was trying to keep an open mind. He also had his notebook and pen ready.

"We're going to discuss how we spend our money using biblical principles. But let me begin by asking you a question about the money you earn. Have you thought about how each of you have been blessed with the talent, intelligence and opportunity to earn the money that you spend?"

As the group considered that question, Pastor Pete continued, "Recall Matthew 6:21." But before he could finish, Geoff chimed in with the verse.

"Where your treasure is, there your heart will be also."

"That's right, Geoff! How we spend our money will determine what our hearts are following. And it will be apparent to us whether we are putting God first in our lives, or whether we are not."

Clapping his hands and then rubbing them together, Mike declared, "Well then, let's begin!"

"Great! But first, we must dispel a few myths about how the world suggests that we spend our money."

Geoff readied his pen, hovering just above his notebook as Pastor Pete continued.

"The first myth that the world believes is that buying things will make us happy. Think about the last large purchase that you made, perhaps new furniture, a vacation or a new car."

Geoff immediately thought about the new Porsche sitting in the Church's parking lot. The Porsche that the Wilsons did not own, as there was an outstanding loan on the vehicle.

"When you think about that purchase today, especially if you had to use debt in the transaction, does it bring you the same happiness that it did on the day you made the purchase?"

Geoff had to admit to himself that it did not. Every time he would get into the car and drive, he was reminded of the large monthly payment required to keep it in their driveway. That was why he and Janice had decided to sell the Porsche and buy a used vehicle.

Pastor Pete's next comment resonated with everyone, especially for one of the participants.

"The second myth is that the more money we make, the more money we should spend on things that we want."

"Ouch!" Mike proclaimed. "That one hits close to home!" Kathy nodded and smiled at her husband.

Pastor Pete continued "When we just consume more because we have the capacity to do so, or we think that we do, it takes us away from our focus on Serving God with Money. We can be deceived by wealth and make possessions our god."

"Any more myths?" Geoff asked.

"One more point I think is worth mentioning is that the world tells us that our possessions define who we are. If we conform to the world as we read in Romans 12:2, we are defined by what we own, rather than WHO owns us – we belong to Jesus Christ, friends. And we should never forget that truth."

Geoff lowered his head and quickly wrote the three myths in his notebook:

THREE MYTHS ABOUT SPENDING

1. **BUYING THINGS WILL MAKE US HAPPY**
2. **THE MORE MONEY WE MAKE, THE MORE WE SHOULD SPEND ON THINGS WE WANT**
3. **OUR POSESSIONS DEFINE WHO WE ARE**

Geoff then started a companion section in his notebook, which he titled "Three Truths About Biblical Spending". He then enumerated the following points:

THREE TRUTHS ABOUT BIBLICAL SPENDING

1. **BUYING THINGS WILL NOT MAKE US HAPPY**
2. **JUST BECAUSE WE MAKE MORE MONEY DOES NOT MEAN WE SHOULD SPEND MORE MONEY**
3. **OUR POSESSIONS DO NOT DEFINE WHO WE ARE, JESUS CHRIST DEFINES US**

Noticing the smile on Geoff's face when he finished writing, Pastor Pete asked "Can you share what you just wrote down, Geoff?"

Geoff looked up and suddenly noticed everyone's attention was focused on him. As he shared his modified list with the group, Janice placed her hand on his arm as if to say: "I'm proud of you."

Pastor Pete sensed this connection and could not hold back a grin. "Given the three points that Geoff has just shared, I would like to follow up with the characteristics of someone who follows Biblical Spending."

Attention turned back to Pastor Pete as he cleared his throat. Geoff put his head down and expectantly awaited the Pastor's next words with his pen ready to write.

"First, a biblical spender is grateful and humble," Pastor Pete began. "The biblical spender expresses their gratitude through humility rather than hubris.

He then opened his Bible and declared "I am going to read for all of you 1 Timothy chapter 6, verse 17:

"Command those who are rich in this present world not to be arrogant nor to put their hope in wealth, which is so uncertain, but to put their hope in God, who richly provides us with everything for our enjoyment."

Geoff captured Pastor Pete's first point in his notebook:

A Biblical Spender is Grateful and Humble.

"Our spending should be guided by gratitude and humility, which means we shouldn't spend in an effort to impress others or to feel secure about ourselves through our wealth."

The room expressed gestures of affirmation, giving Pastor Pete confirmation to continue.

"Many of us probably know someone who has wealth, but instead of expressing gratitude and exhibiting humility, they view their wealth as a source of power. It gives them comfort to exude arrogance in every social setting."

Pastor Pete looked around the room, and as there were no questions or comments forthcoming, he continued.

"Second, a biblical spender is content regardless of their wealth. Recall what the apostle Paul wrote in chapter 4 of his letter to the Church in Philippi."

Geoff's face scrunched as if to communicate his lack of knowledge of the particular passage referenced by Pastor Pete.

"Let me read it for everyone," Pastor Pete offered as he opened his Bible to the chapter in Philippians.

"I rejoiced greatly in the Lord that at last you renewed your concern for me. Indeed, you were concerned, but you had no opportunity to show it. I am not saying this because I am in need, for I have learned to be content whatever the circumstances. I know what it is to be in need, and I know what it is to have plenty. I have learned the secret of being content in any and every situation, whether well fed or hungry, whether living in plenty or in want. I can do all this through him who gives me strength."

There was a brief pause before Janice provided her own insight. "As I think of all that the apostle Paul went through to spread the Gospel, these words amaze me. I don't know how to live up to his embodiment of what it means to be content."

Pastor Pete offered reassurance "Well, Janice, we don't have to face the extremes that Paul faced, living in plenty or in want, whether well-fed or hungry. We just need to make prudent financial choices when faced with these decisions."

"Such as?" Kathy inquired.

"Such as how often to eat out for instance. Families that eat at home can save at least twice as much money and potentially as much as five times their money by cooking and eating at home."[4]

Jaws dropped around the room, especially Geoff's jaw. "I knew you could save money by cooking at home, but I didn't realize how much you can save!"

He then picked up his pen and opened his notebook to record this second characteristic of biblical spenders.

A Biblical Spender is Content regardless of Their Wealth

Waiting for Geoff to finish, Pastor Pete then rounded out the list of biblical spending characteristics. "My

---

[4] CNET: "How much cheaper is cooking at home than eating out?" by Pamela Vachon, May 4, 2023

third and final point is that a biblical spender pursues and achieves freedom from the shackles of debt."

It was evident from the smiles around the room that the thought of being 'unshackled' from their debts gave them a wonderful feeling inside.

With a finger pointed in the air for emphasis, Mike declared "And we've already talked about Smashing Down our respective 'Debt Stacks!'"

As Mike was authoring his announcement, Geoff enabled his pen and wrote this third point into his notebook:

A Biblical Spender Pursues and Achieves Freedom from the Shackles of Debt

While noting the enthusiasm exuding from Mike, Pastor Pete nonetheless wanted to ensure that this point was not lost on everyone.

"The takeaway from this point is not only to BECOME free from debt, but to utilize your Ark Account and Biblical Spending to REMAIN free from debt!"

Tina asked a follow up question "Are there any principles that can help us make biblical spending decisions?"

"I'm glad you asked, Tina!" Pastor Pete enthusiastically responded. "I'm sure that you are all familiar with the Parable of the Talents?"

The participants all nodded to confirm their familiarity, but Mike decided to verbally respond "I love that story, Pastor!"

"And why is that, Mike?"

"Because it's all about money!" Mike gestured by rubbing his fingers together as he responded to Pastor Pete's question.

"Actually, there are a lot of applications for this teaching of Jesus, including one of 'Biblical Spending'".

The group was transfixed on Pastor Pete as he explained how the Parable of the Talents could guide Christians' spending.

"As you know, there are three servants, two who put the talents of the master to work and multiply the master's wealth."

"A great return on investment indeed!" Mike added.

"But the third servant just buried his talent. He didn't use it all, wiping his hands of dirt and the responsibility entrusted to him. The third servant decided to forego investing the talent, one that came with an opportunity cost."

"An opportunity cost?" Fred asked.

"Yes," Pastor Pete responded. "It's an economic concept. An opportunity cost represents the desirable benefits someone foregoes by choosing one alternative instead of another. You might not know with certainty the cost of alternative opportunities, but when you make a purchase, you give up the opportunity to do other things with that money, including saving and investing the money."

"So that's how the parable is tied into biblical spending!" Kathy remarked. "We need to assess the opportunity cost of every purchase, or we might end up just burying that money in the ground if we make unwise decisions."

"Indeed" Pastor Pete responded. "It doesn't mean that you never make another purchase, but you have to weigh that purchase against a variety of other alternatives. And one of the best practices when you are ready to make a major purchase is to wait to act for two to three days after the decision. If you are still in the mode that you want to make the purchase, and you don't have to go into debt to do it, then you should feel comfortable making that purchase decision."

Even Geoff had to admit that his spending habits rarely considered the opportunity cost of trading money for each purchase that he made. He added one more note to his list regarding the concept of opportunity cost and sat back arms-length away from the table to review what he had just written.

CHARACTERISTICS OF A BIBLICAL SPENDER

1. **A Biblical Spender is Grateful and Humble**
2. **A Biblical Spender is Content Regardless of Their Wealth**
3. **A Biblical Spender Pursues and Achieves Freedom from the Shackles of Debt**
4. **A Biblical Spender Assesses the Opportunity Cost of Every Purchase**

"Before we close our session today, I want you all to know that next week we will be discussing Biblical Giving. We will look at the biblical support for being a cheerful giver, and how to think about giving from a biblical perspective."

Geoff audibly groaned, which was only slightly perceptible to the group. However, Janice glanced at him and gave him a brief smile, as if to reassure him that the Wilsons had come a long way. Geoff returned a smile and nodded.

"We'll be here next week, Pastor Pete!"

CHAPTER

14

BIBLICAL GIVING

As the following week progressed, Geoff became increasingly uncomfortable with the topic for the following Sunday's seminar. As the weekend approached, the Wilson family was busy attending Kayla's early season soccer game and then made a trip to Cleveland to watch Stephen's baseball team play in a tournament. Geoff realized that it was time to share his feelings with Janice.

"I just can't shake this idea that this seminar is about increasing our giving to Living Water Church," he admitted on the car ride home from Cleveland. The hum of the couple's 'new' car, a four year old Toyota Rav 4, provided background noise to the conversation. "I think we're making great progress, but in the end, I suspect that we will be told that we have to hit the 10% 'tithe bogey', like it says in the Bible."

"I understand," Janice reassured him. "But you're still open to the idea of what 'Biblical Giving' means for us, and for all Christians, yes?"

Janice's question brought the discussion to the decision point. With a sigh and a thin smile, Geoff nodded and verbalized his commitment. "Yes, I'm open to the idea, Janice. And yes, I'm attending the seminar on Sunday."

Sunday morning arrived, and the Wilson family traveled to Church together. After worship ended, the couple gathered in their usual conference room for the 'Biblical Giving' portion of the Serving God with Money seminar.

Pastor Pete entered the room with his usual positive energy and dove right into the topic for the week.

"I want to begin by asking you a question. What do you think are the biblical reasons for giving?"

The group looked around at each other, but Janice decided to break the silence.

"God has given so much to us, and we should return what He asks."

"That's a great reason, and one that I was going to mention!" Pastor Pete responded. "We should emulate the generosity that God has given to us, as we are implored in Paul's letter to the Church of **Ephesus,**

chapter 5, verse 1: "Follow God's example, therefore, as dearly loved children."

Fred urged the Pastor to continue "What other reasons exist?"

"Well, Fred," Pastor Pete replied. Another reason is that giving with a pure heart and a desire to serve God allows us to store up treasures in heaven. We read this in Matthew 6:21."

"And so, the alternative is to…what?" Geoff countered.

"Well, recall that in a couple of verses earlier in Matthew 6, we are warned by the Gospel writer: 'Do not store up for yourselves treasures on earth'. These verses offer a comparison of the transient wealth offered by the world to the eternal wealth found only in heaven."

"What if we don't feel that we can give right now because we have too many other 'obligations'?" Tina inquired, temporarily shifting back into her more bashful personality.

"That's actually another reason TO be a biblical giver, Tina." Pastor Pete responded.

Tina gave Pastor Pete a quizzical look, and so he explained to the group "Giving is, fundamentally, an act of faith in God. Trusting in our Heavenly Father to meet our needs might seem like a large sacrifice, but we should be reminded of Christ's unfathomable sacrifice for us."

"Are there any examples of this reason for biblical giving in the Bible?" Mike asked, trying to understand the justification from a human perspective.

"Indeed," Pastor Pete replied. "We find an incredible example of trusting God through our biblical giving in Luke chapter 21."

The group opened their Bibles, and as she found the passage before anyone else, Kathy began to read aloud.

"As Jesus looked up, he saw the rich putting their gifts into the temple treasury. He also saw a poor widow put in two very small copper coins. 'Truly I tell you,' he said, 'this poor widow has put in more than all the others. All these people gave their gifts out of their wealth; but she, out of her poverty, put in all she had to live on.'"

Janice began to audibly reminisce aloud, "I remember this passage from my younger days in youth Bible study. I felt sorry for the widow but never thought about the possibility that her faith was so strong that she could give away 'all she had' and just trust God with everything else."

"Thank you for sharing, Janice," Pastor Pete said. "It is indeed a challenge to all of us as we consider how to emulate this widow's faith in God."

"Is this asking us to give all of our hard earned money to the Church?" Geoff questioned with a chuckle. However, behind the frivolity was a real interest in hearing the answer to the question.

"Of course not, Geoff" Pastor Pete responded. "We will talk in a minute about how we put 'biblical giving' into action, but our model is the early church and how they treated their possessions."

Geoff had a puzzled appearance on his face, and so Pastor Pete made a request. "Would you read Acts chapter 4, verses 32-35 for us, Geoff?"

"Be happy to do so" Geoff responded, and after a few minutes of turning the pages in his Bible, found the book of Acts. "Ah, the book of Acts is still after the Gospels!" Geoff's attempt at humor appeared to succeed, with smiles and giggles shared around the room.

"All the believers were one in heart and mind. No one claimed that any of their possessions was their own, but they shared everything they had. With great power, the apostles continued to testify to the resurrection of the Lord Jesus. And God's grace was so powerfully at work in them all that there were no needy persons among them. For from time to time those who owned land or houses sold them, brought the money from the sales and put it at the apostles' feet, and it was distributed to anyone who had need."

When Geoff finished reading the passage, Pastor Pete surveyed the room. While the rest of the group remained silent, reflecting on the passage, until Fred offered a poignant point. "If every church member took this passage to heart, Pastor Pete, many Churches would not be in a difficult financial position."

"Indeed, and it reminds us that Jesus wants us to support those financially less advantaged than ourselves. And note this folks: It's not a suggestion, it's a command."

"He teaches this in Matthew 6:2, where Christ said, 'So when you give to the needy, do not announce it with trumpets, as the hypocrites do in the synagogues and on the streets, to be honored by others.' It emphasizes WHEN we give, not if, and it also chastises those who give only to be seen doing so."

Janice offered her opinion as well. "And if we are indeed a church 'family', then we should be there for one another."

"That's right!" Pastor Pete exclaimed. "In fact, Janice, you have hit on the main reason that we are teaching this seminar. We need to follow biblical financial principles explicitly so that we can help others when called upon to do so by God," he added.

Pastor Pete glanced at his watch, and noting the time, suggested that a recess was in order.

"Now, let's take a short break and come back to discuss how we can put Biblical Giving into action," he said.

Geoff took this opportunity to open his notebook so that he could enumerate the reasons for Biblical Giving that Pastor Pete had just taught the group:

REASONS FOR BIBLICAL GIVING

1. **WE SHOULD EMULATE THE GENEROSITY THAT GOD HAS GIVEN TO US.**
2. **GIVING WITH A PURE HEART AND DESIRE TO SERVE GOD ALLOWS US TO STORE UP TREASURES IN HEAVEN**
3. **GIVING IS, FUNDAMENTALLY, AN ACT OF FAITH IN GOD**
4. **GIVING REQUIRES US TO ASSIST ONE ANOTHER AS A CHURCH FAMILY**

Geoff closed his notebook and placed his pen on the desk beside it. It was time to join the rest of the group for a short break.

CHAPTER

15

BIBLICAL GIVING IN ACTION

A few minutes later, the group reconvened in the conference room. Pastor Pete instructed the couples, saying, "Let's open our Bibles to **Exodus 34:26**. Would someone like to volunteer to read this verse for us?"

In an effort to prove to Janice his high engagement level, Geoff raised his hand to volunteer. He quickly found the verse in his Bible and began reading:

"You shall bring the very first of the first fruits of your soil into the house of the Lord your God."

After a moment to reflect upon the verse, Pastor Pete asked, "What do you think the author of Exodus meant by the term 'first fruits'"?

"Doesn't the verse mean that we should focus on tithing?" Kathy asked. There seemed to be agreement around the table.

Pastor Pete confirmed, "The Old Testament did speak to this idea of tithing and defined tithe as one-tenth of the harvest, or first fruits. But this also applied in other ways. For instance, Abraham offered one-tenth of the spoils of his army's victory in **Genesis 14:20**."

After a pause, he continued, "The concept of tithing is also defined as one-tenth of all blessings, grains and fruits, in **Leviticus 27:30**."

Kathy smiled, feeling justified by her response. But Pastor Pete was about to change the group's perspective on Biblical Giving.

"However, while the New Testament mentions giving in several passages, it does not set a specific amount or percentage. The concept of giving to the Kingdom of God in the New Testament is different."

"How so?" Fred inquired.

"Why don't you tell us Fred, if you would please read next, from **2 Corinthians 9, verses six and seven**."

Fred turned the pages of his Bible to the passage and began:

"Whoever sows sparingly will also reap sparingly, and whoever sows bountifully will also reap bountifully. Each one must give as he has decided in his heart, not reluctantly or under compulsion, for God loves a cheerful giver."

"So, there is no hard and fast rule, according to the New Testament?" Janice voiced the surprise that others in the room were thinking.

"Not when it comes to a specific amount," Pastor Pete replied. "The amount is not the focus in the New Testament. Biblical Giving is as much about our attitude as it is about any fixed rule about how much to give. When we recognize what blessings God has provided for us, our response should be an attitude of gratitude."

Geoff opened his notebook and memorialized these two contrasting views of Biblical Giving:

THE OLD TESTAMENT DEFINES GIVING AS A TITHE (OR ONE-TENTH)

THE NEW TESTAMENT DEFINES GIVING AS COMING FROM THE HEART AND DONE IN A CHEERFUL MANNER

Pastor Pete paused for a moment before he continued.

"However, the giving concept in the New Testament stretches beyond financial giving. This is evident from Paul's letter to the Church in Rome. **Romans chapter 12** begins with Paul imploring the church to 'give their bodies as a living sacrifice', and thus it goes beyond just tithing to include sharing of both our time and talents as well."

This last statement caused Geoff to stop for a second. In that moment, he realized as he reflected on his life that he wasn't focused on fully utilizing his time, talent and treasure as Biblical Giving demanded of him.

"I have to figure out how I can give more, and not just money." Geoff concluded to himself.

Pastor Pete continued, "Although there is no set amount in the New Testament, the tithe of the Old Testament can still be used as a benchmark. It can help you determine the financial level of giving that is appropriate for you.

If you return to your percentages of giving that we calculated when we looked at Biblical Budgeting, you can compare that percentage to both the tithe of 10% and your own personal belief about what this percentage should be. How do you feel about your Biblical Giving in this context?"

"I feel that our giving is not enough," Kathy admitted. "We've never really focused on it before, it just sort of, well, happened."

"Thank you for sharing that, Kathy," Pastor Pete replied warmly. "My hope and prayer for each of you is that you will see this seminar as one way to be intentional about your finances. This intentionality should be practiced across Biblical Budgeting, Spending, Giving, Saving and Investing."

"Did someone say… Investing?" Mike chirped.

"Patience, Mike," Pastor Pete said with a grin. "We're getting to that soon. And while many Christians might think that the lack of a specific percentage in the New Testament is a reason to give less, there is a powerful biblical argument that substantiates why we should give MORE."

Janice quickly chimed in "What verse?"

Pastor Pete quoted **2 Corinthians 8:9** from memory for the group: "For you know the grace of our Lord Jesus Christ, that though he was rich, yet for your sake he became poor, so that you through his poverty might become rich."

The group spent a few moments in quiet contemplation before Pastor Pete summarized the verse.

"Since Jesus gave us everything in order that we may be 'rich' in terms of eternal life, our Biblical Giving should reflect our thanks for His sacrifice for each of us."

"I agree, Pastor Pete," Fred responded. "But how can we get better at 'Biblical Giving'?"

"Well, today's starting point for each of you is your current percentage. The simplest way to increase your giving is in a deliberate fashion. I call it the 'Step Up' Plan to Biblical Giving."

"How does it work?" Geoff inquired.

"Well, you have to commit to gradually increasing your overall giving by a certain percentage over a certain time period. For instance, if you are at 3% of your income today and over the next 7 years you want to be at 10%, simple math would suggest that you increase your Giving by 1% per year. That is, you consistently 'Step Up' by that one percent."

Geoff opened his notebook, but this time he did not plan to take notes. Instead, he drew a staircase and placed the percentage on each stair, increased by 1% per step. Turning the notebook around for everyone to see, Geoff seemed proud of his rudimentary artistry:

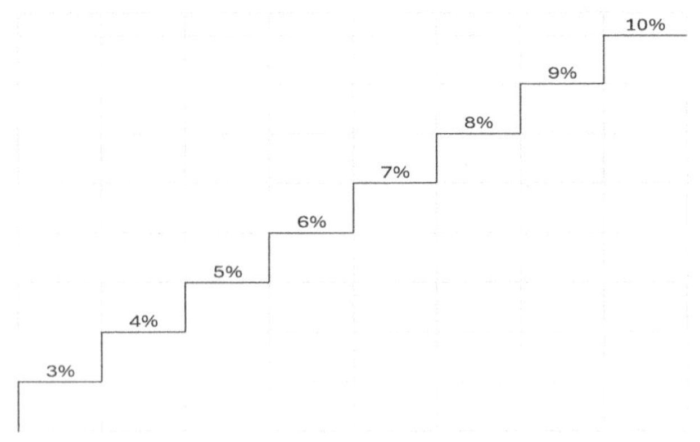

For a copy of this Step Up Exhibit, please visit our companion website:

www.ServingGodwithmoney.org

"This is excellent, Geoff!" Pastor Pete praised.

"While these percentages are incremental, they provide the framework to implement the 'Step Up' plan. But the percentages and number of steps will be different for most couples."

"I like Geoff's drawing, if only because it's easy to understand and calculate how much you plan to 'Step Up' your giving each year" Tina observed.

Pastor Pete nodded approvingly at Tina's use of the phrase 'Step Up'.

"But how do we make this 'Step Up' plan our own?" Kathy asked.

"By using the SMART goal setting process, Kathy."

Having encountered this process in his business career, Geoff interjected. "Yes, our individual 'Step Up' plan should be Specific, Measurable, Achievable, and… I forgot the rest."

"You were close, Geoff!" Pastor Pete then offered the final two words of the SMART process "Relevant, and Time-Specific."

Geoff hit his head with the palm of his hand, eliciting a chuckle from the group. As the laughter died down, Pastor Pete reached into his folder and distributed an exhibit around the room.

For a copy of this SMART Stewardship Form, please visit our companion website: www.ServingGodwithmoney.org

Across the top of the page read 'SMART Stewardship.' Under the heading were each letter of the word SMART with a definition and an area to write one's own notes.

"I urge each of you to sit down as a couple and discuss this exhibit together. Take some time to figure out your own SMART process. From there, you can create your own 'Step Up' plan for your Biblical Giving.

Pastor Pete checked his watch and realized that their time together was at an end. After the closing prayer, the families said their goodbyes until the following Sunday.

"We're going to talk about Biblical Investing next Sunday, right Pastor Pete?" Mike inquired.

"Indeed, we are, Mike."

CHAPTER

16

BIBLICAL SAVING AND INVESTING

The following Sunday, Geoff and Janice entered the Sanctuary prior to Worship. Almost immediately upon sitting down in the pew, Geoff felt a hand on his left shoulder.

"Are you excited about today's session?" Mike simultaneously questioned and declared.

Looking a bit sheepish, Geoff could not dampen Mike's enthusiasm even with his curt response.

"Yes, Mike. I am."

"Me too! I can't wait!"

After worship, Mike bolted out the door and down the corridor to their usual meeting room, leaving Kathy well behind him.

"He's been talking about today's session all week." Kathy admitted to Janice as they gradually made their way to the meeting room.

Once inside the room, everyone made themselves comfortable as Pastor Pete entered.

"I'm hoping that all of you are ready to discuss Biblical Saving and Investing today!"

"We can't wait!" Mike exclaimed.

"First, I want us to discuss how people perceive Biblical Saving and Investing. There are three general philosophies in the Bible." As he said this, Pastor Pete reached into his folder and distributed an exhibit of these philosophies, which read:

God will provide whatever we need.

It is not biblical to save and invest.

It is biblical to save and invest.

"Let's examine these three philosophies together, shall we?" Pastor Pete then read the first philosophy "God will provide whatever we need."

"This philosophy is based on **Isaiah 46:4**, where God tells Isaiah that He will carry, sustain and rescue us."

"But it doesn't mention anything in this verse about our finances, Pastor Pete" Mike noted to the group.

"No, it goes beyond just our physical needs and speaks to a spiritual sustainment. It is also a warning not to worship earthly gods made of gold."

Pastor Pete paused and confirmed the group understood before continuing.

"And it gets at the very heart of our seminar. We can't serve both God and money. That's why we must ask God how we should serve Him WITH our money."

"So does this philosophy run counter to the other two?" Kathy asked.

"It does if it is interpreted to mean that we should ignore our financial stewardship, and that we shouldn't consider the financial blessings that God has given us. But in this context, it is a warning against that behavior and thus does align, as it should, with the other financial teachings of the Bible."

"Well, I'm noticing that the other two philosophies are at diametric odds with one another!" Mike pointed out to the room.

"Yes, and the main reference for not saving and investing are two verses from Matthew's Gospel which we have already read."

Pastor Pete opened his Bible to **Chapter 6 of Matthew and read verses 19 and 20** for the group to hear again:

'Do not store up for yourselves treasures on earth, where moths and vermin destroy, and where thieves break in and steal. But store up for yourselves treasures in heaven, where moths and vermin do not destroy, and where thieves do not break in and steal.'

"Don't these two verses tell us not to serve money, but to serve God?" Janice questioned.

"Of course, Janice!" Pastor Pete responded. "We cannot serve money as an idol. Our intention with Biblical Saving and Investing should be to ensure that we have sufficient means to support ourselves and our families. But it should also warn us against the dangers of debt, of spending beyond our means, and the most important thing about our seminar."

The group leaned in as Pastor Pete's final words completely caught their attention.

"Serving God with money means that you are always ready to help others and also to help the Kingdom of God with your money. When others are in financial difficulty, you can step in and step up. You can then teach them what the Bible truly says about money and help them serve God with their money as well."

"When a missionary trip requires financial support, you are ready to do so. When someone is struggling with a car repair and they need their car to commute to work, you are able to get them past a temporary problem.

When someone is hungry and needs food, you are ready to provide them with assistance."

"But you've missed something, Pastor Pete." Geoff noted. "Where does the Bible justify Biblical Saving and Investing?"

"Ah yes, thank you Geoff. We have many verses that guide this approach."

"Beginning from Genesis chapter 41, Pharaoh is having dreams that he cannot interpret, so young Joseph is brought before him. Joseph informs Pharaoh that only God can interpret his dreams, and that Pharaoh must do as God instructs. After seven years of abundance, a famine will come. Therefore, Pharaoh should save one-fifth of the harvest each year and store it for when the famine arrives. Pharaoh places Joseph in charge of Egypt, and eventually Joseph's brothers travel to request that Joseph assist the land of Canaan."

"So, it is just like serving God with money, but they are talking about grain and not dollar bills?" Mike concurrently asked and stated.

"Yes, it is. Joseph's appointment by Pharaoh was all part of God's plan for him. And God's plan for us regarding our finances is to Biblically save and invest. Then, we can help those less fortunate when God calls upon us to do so, when He presents us with the opportunity."

"And if we don't take that opportunity, we've buried it in the ground, right?" Fred suggested.

"Indeed, Fred! There is a parallel here to the Parable of the Talents."

"What other biblical guidance exists?" Tina asked.

"Well, several Proverbs provide great wisdom regarding financial management. Proverbs 6:6-11, Proverbs 21:5 and 21:20 all offer great financial guidance."

"However, there is a direct resolve to save that is provided in Paul's letter to the Church at Corinth. In 1 Corinthians 16:2, we read this instruction." Pastor Pete turned the pages of his Bible and landed on the aforementioned verse:

'On the first day of every week, each one of you should set aside a sum of money in keeping with your income, saving it up, so that when I come no collections will have to be made.'

"This instruction by Paul is a directive to support the work of the early Church, but growing the church today has its own challenges. And some of them can be supported financially, such as missionary trips to spread the Word of God to impoverished countries through good deeds."

"Well, I'm convinced," Mike declared

Tina asked, "But what practical guidance is available to practice Biblical Saving and Investing?"

Tina's inquiry made Pastor Pete recognize it was time to shift the group's focus to practical investing teaching.

CHAPTER

17

BIBLICAL SAVING AND INVESTING IN ACTION

"I would like to ask a question for each of you to consider," Pastor Pete stated as he handed out another exhibit from his folder.

"Which of the following two scenarios do you think would prove more fruitful in the long run?"

OPTION #1: Investing $3,000 per year for 15 years, earning 8% per year with no additional investment

OR

Option #2: Waiting for 15 years and then investing $6,000 per year earning 8% for 30 years

"That's a great question!" Mike responded while rubbing his hands together. "So, Pastor Pete, the return is 8% per year in both scenarios?"

"Yes."

Geoff thought to himself: I didn't know math would be involved. I should have brought my calculator with me.

Before Mike could provide a response, Tina jumped in with her selection. "I would choose to invest twice as much money each year over a longer period of time. I choose option number two."

Fred added, "I'll go along with my wife and choose option two."

Janice had made her decision. "I think it's option number one, but I don't really have a solid argument regarding my choice."

Geoff put his hand over Janice's on the desk. "I'll go with Janice and choose option one."

Kathy simply stated: "It's option two for me."

Mike sat there silently. Would he support his wife's choice or go out on a limb?

"I pick… option one." Mike said in an uncharacteristic humble and less confident tone. Kathy glanced at him but remained steadfast in her selection.

"Well?" Mike inquired, "Am I right?"

"Indeed, you are, Mike. Option one is the better option." He celebrated by pulling his arm to his side and exuding a confident "YES!"

"But how can this be, Pastor Pete?" Tina inquired.

"Well, option one invests a smaller amount of capital, but at a much earlier time. This gives this money the opportunity to compound to a much higher value before someone adhering to option number two even begins to invest."

Pastor Pete pulled out another document from his folder and distributed the analysis of these two options to the group. One column was labeled 'Earl' and the other 'Lateisha'.

"Clever!" Janice remarked upon seeing the names, quickly associating them with being "early" and "late" to saving and investing.

The results on the page spoke volumes. 'Earl' invested much less money and then stopped investing altogether after 15 years. Yet, he still had a higher investment portfolio value than 'Lateisha' after 45 years of investing.

"OK, Pastor Pete. We get it – invest early and often, yes?" Mike smugly expounded as he looked around the room. Geoff concurrently wrote this point into his notebook:

INVESTING AS SOON AS POSSIBLE AND ON A REGULAR BASIS

"That's certainly one of the main points, Mike. Let me ask you a question, however. Seeing this analysis should inspire everyone to begin investing as soon as possible. So, why don't they do so?"

Mike pondered on the question for a moment. "I assume that they just don't have the capital, the time or the interest?"

"Possibly, yes. But another reason is their belief that unless they have a lot to invest, there is no reason to begin early with such a small amount."

"But how much is enough to get started?" Tina questioned.

Pastor Pete gave her a smile. "Any amount is enough, Tina. You can invest gradually, little by little, and with God's Blessings it will grow over time to a much larger amount. At least, historically, the markets have grown over the long term."

"There's nothing in the Bible about investing even a small amount, though. Is there?" Fred asked.

"Thank you, Fred," Pastor Pete responded. "You have reminded me that I wanted to ask our group another question along those lines. Can you think of anything in the Bible that started small but then multiplied through the miracle of God's blessing?"

After some thought, Janice shouted, "I know, the feeding of the five thousand!"

"Right!" Pastor Pete confirmed. "The feeding of the five thousand is poignant because a young man's modest lunch was able to feed so many people. Christ blessed the meager fish and bread, and the resulting bounty was able to feed everyone until they were satisfied."

"Isn't that the only miracle of Jesus that is recorded in all four Gospels?" Kathy inquired.

"Yes, it is Kathy! And it highlights the point that we should save and invest and ask God in prayer for blessings to multiply our efforts. We see this also in the Parable of the Talents, which we have already discussed."

"Did you know it's my favorite parable?" Mike added.

"I do, Mike. The two 'good and faithful servants' multiplied what the master entrusted them with. The wicked servant buried his talent in the ground, and so it didn't grow at all."

"Therefore, we should take away the lesson to invest like 'Earl' and start as soon as possible, even if the amount is not large."

"What's the best way to do that?" Geoff questioned.

"One great way to get started is to participate in your company's retirement plan, such as a 401(k) plan. Usually, the company will match a portion or all of your contributions up to a certain percentage. This is an example of multiplying our investments without even trying!"

"I'm not sure why everyone doesn't take advantage of their company's retirement plans?" Tina queried.

"Most people would prefer to spend the money, but by adhering to a 'Biblical Spending' mindset, we can ensure that we make full use of any company's retirement plan. Not all companies offer such a plan, so if not, you have to ensure that you save on your own."

"But we don't get a 'match' as you describe it if we do it ourselves?" Fred asked.

"Correct, but IRS regulations allow you to save for retirement on your own. The good news is most companies do offer a plan, and some are automatically enrolling new employees into their plan."

As Pastor Pete paused, Geoff took the opportunity to pick up his pen and recorded this point in his notebook:

EVEN A SMALL INVESTMENT CAN GROW THROUGH GOD'S BLESSINGS OVER TIME

Pastor Pete then shifted the conversation away from retirement investing. "Another way is to invest on your own with excess savings over time. Having a personal investment portfolio in addition to your retirement portfolio should be a part of your plan to ensure that you are maximizing your Biblical Investing opportunities."

"But exactly how do we go about investing, Pastor Pete? Do you have any hot stock tips?" Fred asked, in a half-joking, yet half serious fashion.

"You should probably seek out a professional investment manager," Pastor Pete responded, nodding his head toward a smiling Mike to his right.

"But the tried and true investment plan that has worked for a long time has been summarized by **Ecclesiastes 11:2**, where we read the following:"

'Give portions to seven, yes to eight, for you do not know what disaster may come upon the land.'

Pastor Pete provided an explanation. "The context of this verse is that of a regional trading marketplace, and the 'Preacher' who wrote this book of the Bible is imploring his readers to follow a valuable lesson of investing. What does he instruct here?"

Clearing his throat, Mike offered his thoughts. "It sounds to me Pastor Pete as if we need to spread out our risk. In investment lingo, the word that should come to everyone's mind is to diversify your investments."

"Yes, Mike. This is a great lesson for how to invest our capital! There is also an undertone of trusting God, something that we must do with everything in our lives, including our investments."

"So… no hot stock ideas then?" Fred reiterated, this time with a smirk on his face and a chuckle.

"Sorry, Ecclesiastes 11:2 is a strong reminder not to follow a 'get rich quick' investment, but rather, trust God, diversify, invest and grow your assets slowly but intentionally over time."

Geoff offered his insight. "The best way to do this that I know of is to invest in your company's retirement plan because you essentially buy investments every two weeks when you receive your paycheck."

"We call that 'dollar cost averaging', by the way." Mike stated in a smug manner. "And it's a great way to manage your risk as efficiently as possible."

Geoff clicked his pen and wrote this piece of investment wisdom in his notebook:

DIVERSIFY YOUR INVESTMENTS SO AS TO MANAGE YOUR INVESTMENT RISK

Noting the time on the clock in the room, Pastor Pete let out a heavy sigh. "Well, believe it folks, this is our final session together. You are all now graduates of our 'Serving God with money' seminar!"

It was as if Pastor Pete had let all of the air out of the room.

"Of course, this isn't the end of our conversations. I encourage you to talk with the other two couples about your progress, encourage and help one another, and we will gather in a few months to gauge how everyone is doing."

With that statement, Pastor Pete closed the final meeting of the seminar in prayer and the couples said their goodbyes. While it was emotional, everyone realized that it wasn't really goodbye, as they would all gather together the following Sunday to worship God together at Living Water Church.

CHAPTER

18

SIX MONTHS LATER

It was the first time in a while as the 'Serving God with Money' seminar group reconvened after Sunday's worship service in their regular meeting room. While the three couples had kept in touch after church services, they had not shared their stories since their seminar with Pastor Pete had ended.

Pastor Pete had reached out to each couple the prior week and invited them to share their stories of applying the seminar's teachings to their financial lives.

After hugs and handshakes were shared, the group sat down around the familiar table. It was apparent that the mood of each couple was very upbeat.

"I'm eager to hear your stories!" Pastor Pete opened the conversation.

"We will share first!" Kathy excitedly offered, as she began the Bennett family update.

"The big news is that I've gone back to work, taking a consulting job in the retail industry. It gives me flexible hours and provides me the opportunity to be there for the kids while bringing in more income."

Mike then added to the story. "And we've used that money to smash down our debt stack! I have also reduced my golf outings, and we will only be taking one vacation next year. Our Biblical Budgeting and Spending have allowed us to increase our Biblical Giving and Investing too!"

"That's so wonderful to hear, Kathy and Mike!" Pastor Pete responded. Fred and Tina, how about you?"

"Well, to be honest we had a bit of a setback," Fred admitted.

"Really? Would you be willing to share with us?"

Tina interjected, "Sure, and it has a happy ending. Three months ago, we had to unexpectedly replace our furnace. In the past, this expenditure would have caused us to go further into debt. BUT..."

Fred continued the story. "We had started our Ark Account, so we were able to use the money we had set aside to buy a new furnace."

"And now," Tina added, "we are busy rebuilding our Ark Account."

"Good to hear! The Phillips family's Ark Account really came in handy, didn't it?"

"Yes, it did!" Tina replied.

"Well, how about the Wilson family? I know that Geoff and Janice have really stepped up their Biblical Giving."

Mike turned to Geoff, apparently eager to hear his update. Pastor Pete nodded toward Geoff as if to encourage him.

"We have also paid down some of our smaller debts." Geoff did not go further, so Pastor Pete added to his comment.

"What Geoff is leaving out is that both he and Janice have been busy during the past few months. Geoff has joined our Church leadership board, Janice has signed up to coordinate our mission trip to the South for hurricane relief efforts, and I'm sure all of you have heard of the newly formed Living Waters Helpers Team."

"Of course!" Kathy acknowledged.

"They're helping our congregation with various tasks, right?" Fred queried.

"Indeed," Pastor Pete replied, nodding toward Geoff to pick up the explanation for everyone.

"Before I committed to attending our Serving God with Money seminar, Janice needed a ceiling light replaced, or so we thought." Goeff looked over at his wife and smiled.

"I was shopping at our local Lowes when I ran into Pastor Pete, and he encouraged me to test out a couple of ideas instead of just buying a new light. It turns out it was only a loose wire, and I was able to fix it myself."

After our seminar, I thought a lot about serving God, and not just with our money. So, with Pastor Pete's endorsement and approval, I worked with our Church Secretary to dig out the "Gifts survey" we all completed last year. Now, I am organizing the free time of those members of our congregation that have, as an actor once said, 'a particular set of skills'."

Pastor Pete interjected, "We are asking our experienced volunteers for the Helpers Team to commit at least one hour a week, but hopefully more, to this effort. And then we provide a schedule for the congregation to sign up, first come, and, not to use a pun, but first 'served' for an available time and project."

Geoff continued "We currently have eight volunteers signed up for skills such as electrical work, plumbing, car repair and even landscaping."

He paused, and then gesturing toward him, Geoff announced "And Mike is considering offering his skills in 'Biblical Investing' to our congregation."

"You know what, Geoff? I'm in!" Mark declared.

"Fantastic!" My hope is to offer this beyond the members of our congregation if we can gain a critical mass of volunteers for this effort. It would be a great way to reach our community!"

"Thanks for sharing, Geoff!" Pastor Pete led the group in a round of applause. "And now, I have one final ask of you. We will be offering our 'Serving God with Money' seminar again next spring and would love to have any of you interested in leading a group to volunteer."

The group immediately affirmed their intention to share what they had learned.

"I would be happy to assist!" Janice replied.

"I can help too!" Tina offered.

"You can count me in too, Pastor Pete." Kathy added.

Fred chimed in, "And Geoff, I will sign up for your group. I'm quite handy fixing things around the house."

With that, Pastor Pete closed the update meeting with prayer, which ended with these words: **"Well done, good and faithful servant!"**

CHAPTER

19

SERVING GOD WITH MONEY IN ACTION

I attend a weekly Tuesday Bible study during my lunch hour. As our Bible study ends each week, our leader Bruce Bickel asks all of us attending the same question:

"What are you going to do about what you have just learned?"

Therefore, I think it is appropriate to pose the same question to you. Did you see yourself in any of the characters of this fable? Were there struggles that each couple faced that resonated with you? Were there any surprises along the way, where Biblical Financial teachings ran counter to your expectations?

If you are like me, when you finish reading a book you take a few moments to ask yourself if you felt the time spent was worth what you got out of the book. I hope that your response to that inquiry is that this story provided you with guidance to serve God with your money, and to put the Biblical teachings of financial management into action in your own lives.

If so, I hope that you will apply what you have just learned and begin a new stage in your financial lives. Living with a Biblical principle on our finances is just one way to serve God.

As Christians, we are to give of ourselves in a variety of ways. We are to give our time, talent and treasure to the growth of the Kingdom. This is our calling as good stewards of God's many blessings in our lives, and a responsibility that I pray all of us take seriously. For in the stewardship of our possessions, we imitate the perfect stewardship that Christ displayed when He gave everything He had for each of us.

While this book focuses primarily on Serving God with our money, my prayer for you is that you are sufficiently inspired to pursue a Christian life that permeates all aspects of your days which God blesses us on this earth.

If you find this book helpful, please lend it to someone in your life, so that a person in your family, your group of friends or a fellow Church family member might also be blessed. In fact, this practice of sharing our blessings should be a consistent and intentional practice for every Christian!

I might also suggest that your Church could benefit from using this book either as a guide for a Bible Study, or perhaps a Stewardship campaign. I know that a lot of our churches (especially our smaller churches, which have a special place in my heart) have faithful givers of time, talent and treasure to the cause of the Kingdom!

My final prayer for each of you is that when you stand before the Glory of our Heavenly Father, you hear those familiar words: **"Well done, good and faithful servant!"**

Amen!

CHAPTER

20

ADDITIONAL RESOURCES

As we close this book, I want to ensure that these biblical concepts of finance do not simply gather dust on your bookshelves. Thus, in an effort to maintain a dynamic and interactive discussion regarding Serving God with Money, I highly encourage each of you to check out my companion website or write me an email:

www.ServingGodwithmoney.org

ServingGodwithmoney@gmail.com

On the website, you will find the exhibits that are referenced in the book and a summary of the relevant points that Geoff wrote in his notebook for each stage of Serving God with Money.

It is also my intention to create a Serving God with Money workbook that can be utilized for both individual and group study, a contact list to remain in touch with you and potentially a podcast to share additional insights into all of these areas of biblical financial management.

But I don't want you to stop with just this book. I strongly encourage you to check out other books from some of the great authors writing on this topic of biblical financial management. I would love to hear any new ideas that you glean from others' work, as I believe that those of us writing on this subject are aligned in our interest. And that interest is promoting the biblical pursuit of financial management in our lives.

May God's blessings shine upon you in all aspects of your Christian witness to Him!

About Kharis Publishing:

Kharis Publishing, an imprint of Kharis Media LLC, is a leading Christian and inspirational book publisher based in Aurora, Chicago metropolitan area, Illinois. Kharis' dual mission is to give voice to under-represented writers (including women and first-time authors) and equip orphans in developing countries with literacy tools. That is why, for each book sold, the publisher channels some of the proceeds into providing books and computers for orphanages in developing countries so that these kids may learn to read, dream, and grow. For a limited time, Kharis Publishing is accepting unsolicited queries for nonfiction (Christian, self-help, memoirs, business, health and wellness) from qualified leaders, professionals, pastors, and ministers.
Learn more at: https://kharispublishing.com/

www.ingramcontent.com/pod-product-compliance
Lightning Source LLC
La Vergne TN
LVHW010621100826
845148LV00014B/3068

* 9 7 8 1 6 3 7 4 6 6 8 7 2 *